S0-BCY-995

ANGRY PEOPLE
IN THE
PEWS

ANGRY PEOPLE IN THE PEWS

Managing Anger in the Church

Leroy Howe

JUDSON PRESS
Valley Forge

BV
4627
.A5
H69
2001

ANGRY PEOPLE IN THE PEWS:
MANAGING ANGER IN THE CHURCH

© 2001 by Judson Press, Valley Forge, PA 19482-0851
All rights reserved.

No part of this publication may be reproduced, stored in a retrieval system, or transmitted in any form or by any means, electronic, mechanical, photocopying, recording, or otherwise, without the prior permission of the copyright owner, except for brief quotations included in a review of the book.

Bible quotations in this volume are from *The Jerusalem Bible,* Copyright © 1966 by Darton, Longman & Todd, Ltd. and Doubleday and Company, Inc. Used by permission of the publisher. *The Holy Bible,* King James Version. The *Good News Bible,* the Bible in Today's English Version. Copyright © American Bible Society, 1976. Used by permission. The Revised English Bible, copyright © Oxford University Press and Cambridge University Press 1989. Used by permission.

Library of Congress Cataloging-in-Publication Data
Howe, Leroy T., 1936-
    Angry people in the pews : managing anger in the church / Leroy Howe.
        p. cm.
    ISBN 0-8170-1410-1 (pbk. : alk. paper)
    1. Anger—Religious aspects—Christianity. I. Title.

BV4627.A5 H69 2001
241'.6—dc21

                                                                2001038721

Printed in the U.S.A.
07 06 05 04 03 02 01
10 9 8 7 6 5 4 3 2 1

To Reiss,
whom God answers
in the joy
of his heart

Contents

Preface

THIS BOOK IS ABOUT FAITH'S POWER TO STEM THE RISING TIDE OF anger now threatening human relationships everywhere. Its central conviction is that the Christian tradition offers a time-tested path to overcoming anger's ravages, in ourselves as individuals and in society as a whole. By following this path, we can learn to deal with our own and others' anger in the manner that God intends for everyone. Because there are angry people in our pews as well as in the communities our churches serve, our first step as Christians toward making the world a less angry place is to make the church a less angry place. The purpose of the following chapters is to help us take this crucial first step.

Chapter 1 introduces the basic premises and outlook of the book, and the contribution our churches can make to helping people everywhere to deal with anger more effectively. Chapter 2 draws upon both modern psychology and the Christian tradition for the purpose of identifying and illustrating the several distinctive ways of feeling and expressing anger—some constructive, some destructive—that are available to us as human beings. Chapter 3 explores what the Christian faith does and does not say about being angry. Chapter 4 offers an overview of how and why we experience anger at all. Its central concern is to show how an appreciation of the process of getting angry can help us work out effective ways of expressing the anger we feel. Chapters 5 and 6 provide concrete guidelines for dealing with the varieties of anger that we encounter in everyday life. Chapter 7 focuses on not-so-normal kinds of anger, which is always difficult to manage and which may require professional help for resolution. The final chapter shows how we can express effectively both our appreciation and support to those whose anger is in the service of truly righteous causes.

Angry People in the Pews can be read for personal and spiritual growth; it can serve as the basis for short courses on anger management; and it can be used in conjunction with training people for the ministry of lay pastoral care in Christian congregations. For this latter purpose, the material complements my earlier book on lay shepherding, entitled *A Pastor in Every Pew: Equipping Laity for Pastoral Care*, which was also published by Judson Press.

Acknowledgments

O
F ALL THE QUESTIONS THAT SEMINARY STUDENTS ASKED ME
during my twenty-nine years as a teacher of theology and
pastoral care, two were especially persistent and difficult.
The first is theological: how can we reconcile God's anger with God's
love? The second is pastoral: can Christians who harbor anger ever
become credible agents of reconciliation to an angry world? I cannot
know whether my responses to these questions helped every student
who asked them. I do know how important the questions became to
the planning of this book.

Writing any book on Christian caring without the nurture
and encouragement of fellow caregivers is difficult to imagine. In
my own case, I do not have to try, thanks to the constant support of a special group of Christian friends who are lay shepherds of First United Methodist Church of Richardson, Texas.
On their own, they gently initiate interested inquiries about how
my writing projects are going, and in response to my frequent
requests for their help, they generously offer me suggestions for
improving what I write. My prayer is that this book justifies in
some measure the hopes for it that these cherished friends have
shared with me.

To Robert Macy and his wife, Jean, I owe a special debt of gratitude for the careful attention they have given to the several drafts of the book. Their comments have helped me greatly to make the chapters clearer than they would be otherwise. To Nancy Howe, I offer my deep respect for her knowledge of how the English language works at its best and a grateful heart for the very considerable editorial skills she contributed to our bringing this book to completion. Our marriage not only survives this joint effort; it thrives in it.

1 Introduction

MOST OF MY CHRISTIAN FRIENDS BELIEVE STRONGLY THAT OUR churches should be places of peace and concord, in which members can deepen in their relationships with God and one another unhindered by the angry conflicts and controversies that so dominate social existence today. Though few of these good friends deny that similar conflicts and controversies persist widely within the church itself, they are deeply chagrined by this fact. They rightly wonder whether such a state of affairs does not erode seriously the credibility of the church's message to a world longing for tranquillity and increasingly less hopeful of ever achieving it. One friend put the issue especially eloquently: *If we who are followers of the Prince of Peace can't stop being angry with each other about so many different things, how can we ever expect other people to act peaceably anywhere?*

It is a good thing that committed Christians can take such an unsparing perspective on the actuality of church life. For the world is filled with people who will be only too happy to take up the perspective for us if we do not embrace it ourselves. Indeed, many already are doing so, and are ready to give up on the church altogether as an agent of reconciliation. Instead of finding wisdom in the Christian tradition for dealing effectively with frustrations, disagreements, offenses, resentments, and hostility—the kinds of overcharged emotional reactions that today put everyone at risk—these critics find in our churches as well as in our communities too many complaining, bickering people for whom staying angry at those who offend them becomes a higher form of righteousness than offering the offending parties genuinely Christian concern, forgiveness, and love.

Three major points govern the organization of the following chapters. The first is that the capacity to feel anger at all is one of God's most precious gifts to us, and therefore that getting angry is a normal and predictable part of our experience and growth as God's creatures. The second point is that though anger sometimes gets out of hand, there is always power available to us for overcoming its excesses and for restoring whatever relationship(s) may be threatened by them. This power is the power of the Holy Spirit, bearing witness to what our Lord Jesus Christ teaches all of his followers, then and now, about the proper role of anger in both divine and human life. The third major point of this book is that God calls each of us to draw upon this power and this teaching, first to deal better with our own anger, and then to help our brothers and sisters in the faith to deal better with theirs. When all followers of Christ finally accept this call and seek to fulfill it faithfully in their own lives, then we will be close to the day when the congregations of which we are a part become the havens of peace for which we so fervently long.

The principal goal of this book is to facilitate the process of church members' becoming more effective ministers to the angry people they encounter in their congregations and beyond. Throughout, I will be emphasizing that dealing with anger from the perspective of our faith tradition can be both a satisfying and effective ministry for both clergy and laymembers alike. At the outset, however, it is important that we acknowledge honestly two especially pertinent difficulties of ministering faithfully to others who are in the grip of one or more kinds of anger. The difficulties can be overcome, but they first must be respected.

The first difficulty is posed by our own reluctance to confront the fact that we, too, get and stay angry more often and for longer than is good for us or for anyone else. However devoted we may be to fulfilling Jesus' commandment to love others as we love ourselves, there are times when our irritation and impatience with even those we love the most can get the better of us. In these situations, what we *should* do is take time to consider our response carefully. Instead, however, we may immediately react with ill-timed and ill-tempered words or actions—usually self-serving and offensive—only to regret what we did and to be filled with embarrassment about it. Instead of letting our anger provide the motivation for working out our frustrations with others in a spirit of openness, understanding, negotiation, and compromise, we turn it into some combination of indignation, closed-mindedness, judgmentalism, and hard-pressed demands—to the detriment of relationships that we are almost always better off with than without.

Learning to express our own angry feelings constructively is the all-important first step in preparing ourselves to help others in their own angry moments. To do this, we must be willing to admit that we have the feelings in the first place, and that sometimes we have just as hard a time controlling them as most people do theirs. Once we make these admissions, however, we are well on the way to a better managing of our anger, and to rendering more effective caregiving to others.

The second difficulty we can expect to encounter when we reach out in ministry to others struggling with anger is that angry people are hard to be around for very long. They make great demands on our patience, and can soon exhaust us, if we are not prepared. In this regard, angry people can sap our resources more easily than, say, the anxious, the grieving, and the confused. Most of us have within ourselves a deep enough reservoir of empathy and compassion to help each other move beyond fears, losses, and perplexity. The reservoir drains quickly, however, around people whose predominant feeling is anger. For all our best intentions to the contrary, we can become frustrated, impatient, and even angry toward them, especially if they are angry with us. What most helps us to remain open and nonjudgmental is keeping in view the widest possible perspective on how and why we get angry in the first place.

It is for this reason that I have placed so much emphasis throughout this book on the importance of *understanding* our many ways of feeling and being angry. Developing such understanding is essential to helping ourselves and others to deal with any kind of anger, whenever that anger becomes a primary stressor in life. If we are to be of help to the angry people in our pews, it will be crucial to keep firmly in mind what lies behind every feeling of anger. Doing so goes a long way toward helping us stay the course when another's anger comes close to being all that we believe we can take.

Our grasp of the roots of anger and of the processes by which anger manifests itself in human experience is what finally makes possible the kind of respect and empathy from which the debilitating effects of our own and others' anger can be overcome. In specific: With understanding comes compassion. With compassion comes healthy relationships in which we can be honest with ourselves and others about our own anger. Understanding and compassion, together, can help us to express our anger more effectively to one another, without putting ourselves and our relationships in jeopardy.

The same understanding that undergirds greater compassion toward angry people on our part, and toward us on their part, also yields safeguards against anger's most destructive forms. However respectful of others we are called to be as Christians, we also are called to be respectful of our own integrity and sense of worth as God's creatures and to exercise appropriate caution when another's anger threatens to compromise either. Though guardedness without respect and empathy will eliminate any possibility of our helping people deal constructively with anger, respect and empathy without caution can put us significantly at risk. Discerning when another's anger becomes dangerous, both to that other and to us, requires more than an otherwise laudable commitment to being empathic and respectful; it requires an appreciation of the dynamics of anger and its aberrant forms, of the sort this book seeks to provide.

In sum: Understanding why and how we get angry, and how to work through our own anger constructively for the sake of more fulfilling relationships, is essential to our developing the empathy and compassion needed to express Christian care to people whose anger is a problem for their everyday living. Such understanding is also important to our learning to distinguish the kinds of angry people we can work with safely from those who need a different kind of help than we can provide. Even more importantly, however, understanding the bases and process of anger will bring us face to face with one of the most important parts of the Christian message: God's desire is that our anger be what our Lord spoke of as "for cause." I will be referring to this kind of anger variously in the pages to follow, e.g., especially as "righteous" anger and as "prophetic" anger.

As the chapters to follow seek to show, it is righteous or prophetic anger that God wants us especially to take seriously, to act upon, and to become agents of reconciliation as a result. Critics of our churches, therefore, are only partially correct when they chide us for bringing too much anger with us to our worship of a God of love. Our problem as a church is not simply that there are a lot of angry people in our pews. It is, rather, that we are carrying around too much of the wrong kind of anger. In specific, many people in our pews suffer from anger mired in purely personal frustrations and an intense sense of entitlement to immediate redress of others' wrongs against them. Instead, what we most need in our pews today are people capable of being inspired by a prophetic zeal for justice, liberation, and love in a world rejoicing in hope. In this kind of anger, there can be new birth for all of us.

2 The Many Faces of Anger

IN SOME PEOPLE, ANGER IS EASY TO MISS. ONLY CLOSE FRIENDS CATCH the ever so slightly downturned mouth and tightened neck muscles that betray the carefully cultivated disguise. Other people leave no doubt about what they are feeling. With red cheeks, bulging eyes, and flaring nostrils, they look like raging bulls eager for confrontation. Just as angry feelings can differ markedly in kind and intensity, the people who exhibit them can appear subtle, overbearing, cloudy, haughty, contorted, fuming, icy, stormy—and more besides. Over one person's countenance, anger passes as if with the blink of an eye; over another's, it freezes into a permanent scowl.

Just as anger has many faces, angry faces provoke different reactions from those who gaze into them. We may become puzzled: *Please, just tell me what I've done.* We may simply want to get away: *When you get that look, all I want to do is run from you as fast as I can.* We may gear up for battle: *Just who do you think you are staring at me with that put-out expression on your face?* We may reach out for reconciliation: *I'm sorry I've been so insensitive to where you are in all this. I guess it took scowling at me to finally get my attention.*

Not surprisingly, we use more than the one word *anger* to describe the several kinds and degrees of irritation and displeasure to which human beings are vulnerable. We also use the words *fury, rage, indignation, wrath,* and *hate.* In this chapter, we will be exploring all of these feelings, as well as the several kinds of choices that people make both to keep such feelings to themselves and to express them to others, constructively as well as destructively. Each section in the chapter begins with a brief vignette from an actual situation (with names and details changed in the interest of protecting privacy) and proceeds by discussing the specific feeling of irritation/displeasure and manner of expressing it that the vignette illustrates. The primary purpose of the discussion is to heighten our understanding of how many ways there are to feel and deal with anger and of how important it can be to our inner well-being and to our relationships that we understand and respect the differences.

MANAGING VERY WELL, ALMOST

Four-deep in the checkout line, Rhea thought to herself how foolish she was for waiting until the busiest time of the week to do her grocery shopping. Patiently, however, she endured the time it took for the three shoppers ahead of her to complete their purchases and be on their way. Then, just as she reached into her cart for the first item, the cashier wearily told her that he was going on break and that the lane would be closed. Rhea felt her displeasure well up strongly within her and for a moment wanted nothing more than to vent it openly. Instead, she reminded herself of her own contribution to her predicament and quietly moved her cart one aisle over (to follow two more people ahead of her). However, as she waited, she continued to harbor antagonism toward the clerk who had cut her off so abruptly.

In this situation, Rhea feels strong irritation but chooses not to express it outwardly. She hides her feeling so well that no one around her senses how out of sorts she really is. In fact, Sue, a neighbor who followed Rhea to the other line, said admiringly: *You are such a patient person, Rhea, so gracious to that young clerk; I was about to give him a good piece of my mind.*

How Rhea handled this particular provocation fully reflects her general attitude toward anger. For her, holding anger in is almost always the best course because, she believes, eventually it will just go away on its own. Though she may be feeling strong displeasure, the face that Rhea shows to others almost always hides the fact that she is angry. In this sense, her face is more like a mask. What lies behind the mask, others can only guess. For example, Rhea's husband complains openly to close friends that he often has a hard time figuring out what his wife is feeling at all. Frequently, he chides his wife for bottling up so much of her anger.

Bottling up anger is as unattractive an option for Rhea's neighbor as it is for her husband, at least if we can believe what Sue said to her in the checkout line. There, Sue talks about getting anger out at its source. Both women feel displeasure and antagonism on occasion, but while Rhea chooses to contain it within herself, Sue prefers to give it outward expression, in a form that all can see. Though Sue is aware that her outspokenness sometimes puts people off, she also believes that for the sake of any kind of relationship, even a purely functional one in a grocery store, the honest sharing of feelings is the best policy.

Among mental health professionals today, the consensus prevails that Sue's way of dealing with anger is healthier than Rhea's. On the whole, the professionals say, it is better to share openly our feelings of frustration, dissatisfaction, and resentment than to keep them to ourselves, for sharing more easily gets to the anger's source. With this prevailing view in mind, let's look again at Rhea. Though the comment by Rhea's husband may reveal more about his own inability to listen well than about her inhibitedness, its surface meaning suggests that Rhea's strategy of containment might be negatively affecting her marriage. Holding her feelings in could have a negative effect both on Rhea's other relationships and on her inner peace. In this regard, it is interesting that among the roots for the English word *anger* are words meaning "narrow" and "strangle."

Clearly, we have reason to question whether Rhea is well served by her general policy of keeping her angry feelings in check. However, expressing anger whenever and however we feel it may not be the best course either. For example, Sue reluctantly admits that her habit of telling people off, whenever she determines that they need to be told, has had more unpleasant consequences for some of her relationships than she would like. Some who have borne the brunt of her bluntness, she says, still remain offended. Sue further concedes that she finds it prudent never to disclose her irritations to some people, namely, her boss, her priest, and her daughter-in-law!

A neighbor of both Rhea and Sue, Belle also knows the grocery store clerk who abruptly cut off Rhea. After hearing Sue's description of what happened in the line, Belle snorted:

Doesn't surprise me a bit. There's always something with that kid. Last time I was in his line, he and the bagger kept talking to each other, and he ran some of my things through twice. It was all I could do to get the manager off the phone to take my complaint. And then that old man who took my groceries out to the car banged the cart against my door. And you'll never guess what happened on the way home after all that!

To everyone who knows her, Belle is a complainer who never forgets a wrong done to her. Everyone who has even a brief conversation with her comes away stunned by how resentful she is of so many people and things that, by her own words, even she cannot count them all. Her approach to angry feelings is quite different from Sue's and perhaps as well from Rhea's. Belle neither works at letting go of her anger nor gives it expression at the time she is feeling it. Instead, Belle harbors grudges.

All of us experience frustrations, dissatisfactions, and irritations that are normal reactions to certain kinds of events. For example:

She walked by me as if I weren't even there.
He keeps borrowing more and more tools without bringing the other ones back.
This is the third time that her kid's baseball has gone through the garage window.

Whichever way we choose to deal with our anger in such circumstances, namely, by holding it in or by letting it out, most of the time we get both the anger and the memory of what provoked it behind us and move on. Belle, however, rarely if ever leaves resentments behind, even when she expresses them to whoever provokes them. As a result, she remains enslaved by them. Her waking moments are filled with festering anger, which she spews out at every opportunity and with the greatest gusto. Belle's chronic anger almost seems to define her very being.

More than likely, the reason that Belle harbors so many grudges and resentments is that she has experienced more than a usual number of offenses, deprivations, and abuses in her life. She may have a lot to be displeased with, irritated about, and antagonistic toward. Nevertheless, many people suffer all kinds of outrages without developing anything like the intense bitterness that so characterizes Belle. Therefore, we must look further for a full explanation of the kind of grudge-anger that she so typifies. Part of the explanation lies with the very friends who never tire of telling others how hard she is to be around but who typically offer Belle too much sensitive and non-judgmental listening, empathizing, and affirming!

Nothing is intrinsically harmful about any of these latter reactions. Indeed, both separately and together, they constitute what most of us would regard as the heart and soul of caring. In Belle's case, however, though well-intentioned, these reactions may be providing just the encouragement she needs *not* to get over her chronic anger. In fact, her incessant exhibitions of letting her anger out impede her from becoming the kind of forgiving and loving person God desires all of us to become. Others' toleration of her histrionic displays may be doing as much for her resentment as oxygen does for a fire.

In summary: Rhea, Sue, and Belle present to us three different, but easily recognizable, faces of anger. The first two express the normal kinds of angry feelings that all of us experience frequently in our daily lives. The third is a little more disturbing, but most of us have harbored at least a grudge or two at sometime or another. What is common to all three is some combination of feeling frustrated, annoyed, irritated, or antagonistic. Rhea chooses to contain these feelings within herself, and hopefully she forgets about what provokes at least most of them. By contrast, Sue lets out her feelings when and where they are aroused in her. Belle, however, chooses merely to dwell on them, allowing them to merge into a permanent state of resentfulness, complaining continuously to all and sundry. Note that in all three, even Belle's, the manifested anger is at a relatively low level of intensity. In the next vignette, the intensity mounts to become a distinguishing feature in itself.

LOSING CONTROL AND LOSING FACE

Bill is proud of his ten-year-old son, Mark, and enjoys being in the stands at Mark's softball games. With two runners on base, Mark is now at bat. He has two strikes and doesn't swing at the next pitch. To Bill, the pitch was wide of the plate. The umpire sees it differently, calling Mark out on a third strike. With temples pounding, face beet red, and arms waving frantically, Bill leaps from his seat, races toward the umpire, and begins screaming at him. Mark is overcome with embarrassment.

This scene would be comical, were it not being repeated on so many playing fields today accompanied by downright frightening displays of aggression. Happily for the umpire, Bill's reaction on this particular occasion is merely fulminating; he makes no physical threats. This umpire has seen it all before, many times over. Although Bill's behavior is hilariously out of proportion to the perceived offense, no one is laughing. Alarmed at himself, Bill confesses that it was all he could do to stop himself from taking a swing at the umpire.

The word *anger* doesn't begin to capture the essence of an outburst like Bill's. *Fury* expresses it better. Feelings of fury have all the previously noted characteristics of anger: displeasure, frustration, irritation, and antagonism. However, two further characteristics distinguish fury from anger: overwhelming intensity and loss of self-control. With the loss of self-control comes the loss, at least temporarily, of the power to choose how we will or will not express what we feel at the moment, leaving us at the mercy of the feeling itself. Rhea, Sue, and even Belle are able to decide what actions they will and will not allow to flow from their respective feelings. At the moment, Bill is unable to make any decisions at all. He is wholly caught up in reacting to a strong feeling within himself that is wildly incongruous with what is actually going on around him.

On a positive note, Bill quickly begins to feel as embarrassed with himself as his son is for him. In fact, just as the word *anger* does not adequately express what fury truly is, the word *embarrassment* does not come close to naming the feeling that gradually overcomes Bill:

I'm so ashamed of myself that I don't think I can ever show my face to these parents again. And most of them are my friends! What am I gonna do? What's wrong with me?

Bill's last question is to the point. For a moment, something *was* wrong, terribly wrong, with, in, and about him. His mounting sense of shame is altogether appropriate, for in his fury, something truly horrific happened to Bill. As Bill describes it: *I just lost it.*

What, specifically, did Bill lose? Most importantly, he lost the sense of connection with a vital part of his humanness, his God-given ability to bring his feelings under the control of his judgment. Momentarily, he became a deranged creature acting on mere impulse, oblivious to any consequences of his actions and ready to do real harm to a fellow human being who instead deserved his support. But Bill's feeling of shame quickly began to do its restorative work of helping him come to terms with his behavior and with himself. He resolved not only to *do* better but to *be* better and to ask many of his friends, as well as the umpire, for their forgiveness and support. Together, he, Mark, and their friends relished a happy ending to a story whose outcome could have been disturbingly different.

Not every furious person is as competent as Bill proved to be in getting his or her act together. That this is so constitutes one of the most pressing problems of today's society. All of us encounter enough furious people in our everyday activities to be deservedly concerned about the increasing possibilities for violence everywhere. No place seems to be a completely safe haven anymore, not even our schools, churches, and hospitals. When anger escalates to a level of intensity that compromises peoples' self-control, anything can happen and, as the next section discusses, frequently does happen.

FROM FURY TO RAGE

Out of the corner of her eye, Patsy could see it coming, but she was unable to do anything to stop it. The pickup truck swerved sharply into her driver's side door, momentarily forcing her car onto the side of the road. As she struggled to get her weaving vehicle back onto pavement, she could see the driver's hand forming an obscene gesture as he sped away. She recognized him as the one who had honked incessantly behind her when they passed through town, insisting that she move before a red light changed to green.

If the many stories we hear and read about road rage are any indication, Patsy probably should count herself blessed that she survived this ordeal at all. Only a few hundred yards ahead, this particular road curves around a steep drop-off that has claimed many drivers over the years. The enraged, violent young man who put Patsy in such danger has no business being on any road in the emotional condition he displayed in this situation. Unfortunately for all of us, however, countless numbers like him are on our roads, and our very next journey may bring us face to face with one of them.

What is strikingly similar about both the truck driver and Bill is the intensity of their respective feelings. However, important differences exist between the kind of anger that Patsy's antagonist displays and the kind that Bill hurled at Mark's umpire. Though both men are overwhelmed with frustration and irritation and do violence to a fellow human being as a result, Bill's blowup goes no further than verbal abuse, while the driver of the pickup sets out to inflict actual physical harm. Bill's fury dissipates almost as quickly as it springs to life, but the truck driver's rage fuels a willful plan of destruction that comes too close to succeeding for comfort. Whereas Bill is ashamed of himself, the truck driver gloats proudly as he speeds away, probably to harass someone else on the road.

Bill's fury is expressed anger run amok. The truck driver's rage is grudge-anger escalated to dangerous levels. Neither is contained adequately, and from neither can anything good come, except through the intervention of a sense of regret and remorse. Mortified, Bill quickly becomes regretful enough to apologize and remorseful enough to begin mending his ways. Though the umpire in particular might have wished that Bill's change of heart had come sooner, he can take comfort in contemplating that now there may be one less angry parent in the stands to worry about. Insofar as it proved to be a catalyst for beneficial change, Bill's tirade seems to have brought about at least some good. We have little reason to be optimistic about a similar outcome in Patsy's case.

As we will see later, the irresponsible driving habits of Patsy's antagonist continue to put others at risk. This young man drives with a sense of entitlement that makes him react instantly and with hostility when anyone else claims any part of the road that he himself may want. For him, because others on the road have no rights in the first place, they have no legitimate claims to make against anything that he may choose to do while behind the wheel. Bent on retaliation for the slightest offense, he is a menace to others and, ultimately, to himself. His, however, is not the only way for anger to become retaliatory, as we shall see in the next vignette.

GETTING MAD AND GETTING EVEN

The lunch was a welcome break from a pressure-filled morning in the office. Frank, Jerry, and Steve shared some of their frustrations, had a few good laughs together, and returned to the "grind" energized for the afternoon's work. During the conversation, Frank and Steve relayed to Jerry, in confidence, some doubts they had about whether their current project could be completed successfully. The next day, their director gave them a dressing down for saying things that could hurt the company. Frank and Steve are both incensed at Jerry's betrayal. Frank vows never again to speak of anything relating to business when Jerry is around. Steve vows to find a way to "return the favor" the first chance he gets.

If this scenario is any indication, Frank shares something in common with Rhea, the prominent character in our first vignette. Though Frank is much angrier with his friend Jerry than Rhea was with the grocery store clerk, he nevertheless handles his anger in much the same way that Rhea did hers. He contains the anger within himself. He does not express it openly to the person toward whom he is feeling it. As a result, Jerry is left to guess whether or not he may have done something to set Frank off. Perhaps Jerry will pick up a clue from Frank's refusal to participate in the sorts of conversations the two previously enjoyed. Whether Jerry does or not, however, a part of his relationship with Frank will change, and Jerry may never know that it is due to Frank's unilateral determination.

We do not know whether Rhea is successful in getting over her anger at the grocery store checker by acknowledging the vulnerability to frustration that her own procrastination had heightened before she ever entered the store. Rhea may decide simply to avoid this particular checker's lane in the future and let it go at that. If avoidance is the course Rhea pursues, then her approach to dealing with anger will come very close to Frank's indeed: hold the anger in but change the terms of the relationship in order to eliminate future anger-producing frustration, at whatever expense to the relationship.

This latter approach is seductive in that it deftly shifts the responsibility for our own anger onto others. By blaming someone else for making us mad, we no longer have to examine the realism of our expectations of others, our own irritability, and our lowered frustration tolerance. We can rest content in the false assurance that when we get mad, it must be somebody else's fault. The problem with taking this approach is that it compromises the core integrity of all healthy relationships, whether they are casual, intimate, or merely functional in nature. That compromise blocks open sharing and the resolving of differences to the mutual satisfaction of all participants. In a healthy relationship, at whatever level of closeness, changes in the terms of the relationship come from mutual deliberating and deciding; they are not imposed by one party onto the other.

Frank seems to believe that since his relationship with Jerry is confined to work, nothing of importance is lost by deciding on his own to relate differently to Jerry in the future. Perhaps he is right in believing so. It might not matter at all to Jerry whether Frank does or does not discuss business with him. However, whatever may be the actual consequences of Frank's unilateral decision, the decision itself conspicuously lacks respect—respect for its possible impact on Jerry, for the integrity of the relationship, for the need all of us have to be forgiven our mistakes and shortcomings, and for the person Jerry is, even if some of Jerry's actions fall short of what Frank would hope to receive from him. Frank's very controlled and controlling way of dealing with anger can weaken many of his relationships, not only the one he has with Jerry.

If Frank's approach to anger bears some resemblance to Rhea's, Steve's position threatens to imitate Belle's. If he really means what he says to Frank, Steve will massage his anger for as long as it takes to make Jerry pay for violating a confidence. Like Belle, Steve plans neither to forgive nor to forget. It remains to be seen, of course, whether

Steve will carry out his threat. If he does, however, he will embark upon a different course than Belle's. While Belle just stays mad, Steve will get even. But Steve might not go through with what he says he is going to do. Certainly, he has other options. He could harbor his grudge indefinitely, as Belle does hers, and gain his satisfaction from constant complaining instead of from taking direct action to make his situation better. Or he could confront Jerry directly over the incident, as Sue might in a similar situation, express his displeasure about the betrayal of confidence, and seek assurances that the offensive behavior will not be repeated. Finally, Steve could resolve to forget about the incident, as if it were of no real consequence, and go on as if it never happened.

Whatever Steve ends up doing in this situation, right now he seems bent on using his anger to empower acts aimed at evening the score. If he carries out this strategy, he will be utilizing a very old approach to dealing with the anger that slights, betrayals, and injuries can arouse in us: retaliation. All over the world, it is common practice never to allow an offense to go unavenged. Optimally, the offending party admits to wrongdoing and voluntarily offers adequate restitution; then the anger harbored by the offended party gradually dissipates. Frequently, however, the optimal solution fails to materialize, and the offended seeks redress on his or her own terms, within or outside of whatever legal system may be operative. For many people, ignoring an offense, letting it pass, and forgiving the offender are not viable options. Either blind anger or some system of equitable justice or both eventually drive them to demand recompense for the particular offense committed and punishment to deter future offenses.

In the interest of a stable social order, the demands of civility narrow the means we may employ to attain from offenders the satisfaction that we think we deserve. For example, ancient Judaism put forth the principle of *lex talionis*, letting the punishment fit the crime (e.g., an eye for an eye), as superior to earlier practices of seeking revenge all out of proportion to damage actually suffered (cf. Lamech's boast in Genesis 4 of punishing his enemies seventy-seven times over). Our own criminal justice system exemplifies the eye-for-an-eye tradition. Though we continue to speak of rehabilitating wrongdoers, we are more interested in ensuring that those who offend and harm us pay dearly for their actions. And in this rests the fundamental problem: neither recompense received nor punishment exacted helps us much to let go of the anger that the original offense arouses in us. Steve may be able to make Jerry pay for his indiscretion, perhaps by slandering him in some way, but he may not find it as easy to get his anger behind him by doing so.

WRATH THAT KNOWS NO END

In spite of all the paramedics' best efforts, Tommy dies on the way to the hospital. His mother, Cindy, arrives at the hospital in another ambulance, shaken up but not injured. She is told the terrible news of her little boy's death as the drunken driver of the other vehicle, who was responsible for the crash, is wheeled into the emergency room for his own treatment. With blazing eyes, Cindy follows the gurney down the hallway and screams: "I'll never forgive you for what you did to Tommy! As God is my witness, I want to make your life a living hell, just like you've made mine."

Venomous as Cindy's rage is, it is not difficult to appreciate it in the situation at hand. The loss she must deal with is both unnecessary and overwhelming, and the only thing that may keep her from being wholly consumed by grief is the rage that she can direct toward the perpetrator of her son's death. Two years following this tragic incident, Cindy is still raging against Tommy's killer. She frequently entertains thoughts of revenge when the man is eventually released from prison. The best word we have in English to name the kind of anger that Cindy feels is *wrath*.

Cindy's friends react in different ways to her struggle for peace of mind. One friend wistfully remembers how things were between them before the accident and wishes only that somehow they could be that way again. Another blames liquor more than the driver for the incident and thinks Cindy has demonized the perpetrator unjustly. Still another believes that Cindy should be coping more actively with her distress by joining an organization such as Mothers Against Drunk Driving. Her pastor supports Cindy's commitment never to forget what happened to Tommy but counsels her to forgive the killer and to be grateful for the time she and Tommy did have together.

Though she would like to add her own punishment of the drunken driver to the state's, Cindy knows that she will never take any of the actions that she fantasizes about. Not the retaliatory kind of anger that we identified earlier in Steve, Cindy's anger exhibits the lingering quality of Belle's grudge harboring and has the kind of intensity that we saw both in Bill and in the pickup truck driver. In the final analysis, though, Cindy's anger has a quite different quality about it than any of the kinds of anger we have discussed thus far. It is intense, sustained, and retaliation oriented but for an indisputably *good* reason. What Cindy is angry about should never have happened, and her intense feeling is thoroughly appropriate to what actually did happen. Cindy's anger is a *righteous rage* that testifies to very real evils that do occur in human experience and that are no respecter of peoples' careful planning, exercise of due caution, or virtue.

Cindy has every right to feel wrathful. Further, she has every right to feel wrathful for a very long time. How angry does she have a right to be? For how long does she have a right to be so angry? From both a psychological and a moral perspective, who among us can say? Given the enormity of the senseless destruction that has struck at the very center of her life, Cindy could decide responsibly to sustain her righteous anger at rage levels even for the rest of her life. Some in her place would choose to do this as a way of honoring the memory of the child cut down before coming even close to attaining the prime of life. Cindy does not have the right to enact vengeance on Tommy's killer directly; only God and the state have the right to do this. But she does have the right to hold on to her anger for as long as she chooses. Cindy's is a principled anger, not merely a mindless reaction all out of proportion to its stimulus. On principle, it is not wrong for Cindy to keep her anger close to the surface of her everyday living and allow it never to slacken.

Should Cindy take this course of action? Psychology, committed as a discipline to the realm of facts and not of values, cannot answer such a question. Moral philosophy can speak to the question clearly and cogently but cannot prescribe any single answer to it. From the standpoint of morality, Cindy's stance toward her son's killer cannot be assessed adequately without taking into account the specific moral commitments Cindy herself espouses. Our faith, however, may be able to shed a different kind of light on the issue than the illumination that psychology and moral philosophy afford us.

From a faith perspective, a crucial distinction exists between protesting another's irresponsibility and making that protest the sum and substance of our existence. All of us are called by God to offer reproof and discipline to those whose actions clearly run counter to God's revealed will, but we are neither authorized nor empowered by our Creator to act on God's behalf in bringing sinners to justice. As James reminds us, "The wrath of man worketh not the righteousness of God" (James 1:20, KJV). Or in the words of the Revised English Bible: "For human anger does not promote God's justice." For the most part, dealing with our own sins is about all that any of us can manage, if that.

Through the ages, however, a small number of men and women, for reasons known only to God, have been called as prophets to bear special and sustained witness to what God expects from all of us and to what happens when we fail to meet divine expectations. We regard these people as having a vocation that encompasses nothing less than the whole of their lives. God calls them to speak zealously, often with indignation at our blindness and hardness of heart. The purpose of their speaking is to bring us to our knees in repentance and in renewed commitment to do all that God asks of us on behalf of a suffering humanity groaning in travail for reconciliation, unity, and peace. For such people, occasional protests against one person's and then another's irresponsibility are not enough; the protesting must be against a wider kind of disorder and must become the sum and substance of their lives.

In the light of this faith perspective, should Cindy continue to make her wrath the sum and substance of her life? Probably not. Her rage, though righteous, is not divinely inspired. It seeks not the repentance but the destruction of the one to whom it is directed. And it is directed only at one person and not a whole community. Will it be helpful if a caregiver says all of this to Cindy directly? Probably not. Hopefully, however, and with much empathetic listening, understanding, and prayer, a faith-guided friend, lay minister, or pastor will be able to lead Cindy to the place where she can make these discoveries for herself and, in the process, discern more clearly what God does intend for her to do with the rest of her life.

HATE

Prophetic anger differs markedly from the kind illustrated in the following vignette:

> They left the young man lying on the side of the road, his body broken from the savage beating. Later, they gleefully recounted their savagery to their friends, who cheered them boisterously between bouts of pouring beer over their heads: "One less fag in the world! Who could ask for a better night than this!"

Much in this vignette provokes and sustains sheer revulsion. The acts alluded to are atrocious, inflicted by despicable men who seem utterly without redeeming features, horrific examples of what human beings can come to in their darkest moments. With no sense of connectedness with the plight of the victim, who may have struggled for years with a form of manhood that alienated him from most of his contemporaries, the killers felt only contempt, not just for the young man as an individual, but for a whole group whom they arbitrarily deem unacceptable. At some other time and place, it might have been an African American so victimized or a Jew or a Tutsi or a Cambodian or. . . . Modern history makes the possibilities almost endless. In every such victimization, the elements are shockingly the same: hostility toward stereotyped differences between people, combined with an audacious and outrageous denial of another group's right to exist. This is the true meaning of hate.

Most basically, hate is the destructive combination of mindless animosity toward groups of people in the abstract, judgment of individual worth solely on the basis of an individual's relation to the disparaged group, and violent acts aimed to wipe the unwanted group off the face of the earth. Hate is the root of every kind of enacted prejudice against any human being anywhere on earth. Wherever and whenever it occurs, our heavenly Father, who continues to create all things and to call them good, is dishonored, to the peril of our very souls. Wherever and whenever hate occurs, Jesus Christ, who came that all might have life in abundance now and forever, is again mocked, scourged, and crucified in our hearts. Wherever and whenever hate occurs, the Holy Spirit, the Comforter and Advocate of everyone, is repudiated in favor of a spirit of divisiveness, aggression, and destruction toward everyone whose loyalties are not with the self-appointed purifiers of humankind's history.

The kind of hate exhibited by the young man's killers is diabolical to the core. What does it mean to say this? The word *diabolical* is often associated with the demonic or the satanic. Any of these three words can be a way of referring to the hovering, threatening presence of evil forces, and perhaps even evil personages, bent on overpowering the benevolent structure and aims of the world created, redeemed, and sustained by our loving God. Indeed, the actions of the men exhibit a demonic quality. One of the ablest lay ministers of pastoral care I know unhesitatingly attributed the terrible scene to the work of the devil. Whether or not we share this particular assessment of the situation, we certainly can agree that the torture and killing of innocent victims is, purely and simply, evil, for which there is no justification, ever.

As thoroughly appropriate as it is to characterize the killers of the young gay man as demonic or satanic (so long as we do not thereby absolve them of responsibility for their actions), there is more to the vignette than this. Consider again the word *diabolical*. The realm of the diabolic is not so much the realm of the legions of Satan as it is the realm of the separated, the divided, the broken up, and the broken apart. At its core, diabolism rips the fabric of the unitive order intended by God. In place of wholeness, diabolism substitutes disparateness. Its love is for the partial, the fragmentary, the piecemeal, the disconnected: *our* family, *our* people, *our* country, *our* way, over against all of yours. Its ultimate distortion is the confusion of one piece of a ripped-apart social order for the whole. Diabolism sustains the distortion by lusting after the destruction of every piece other than the ones to which it desperately clings. Prejudice, ethnic cleansing, totalitarianism, and exclusivism are all diabolical in nature and rest upon the all-too-frequently unacknowledged foundation of hate.

Everything that God seeks to join together, diabolism strives to put asunder.

Hate divides, but it does not conquer. It only engenders more hate, a feeling that can hold people in its grip over many generations and many centuries, immersing them in conflicts without end, bereft of any meaningful hope that anything might ever be different. The destructive power of hate is truly awesome. We cannot challenge it successfully by treating it lightly.

SUMMARY

In this chapter, we have looked across a wide spectrum of angry feelings that vary considerably in intensity, duration, felt importance, manner of expression, and effect on others. We have also discovered that there are many ways of dealing with these feelings. At one extreme, we may choose not to show displeasure at all. At the other extreme, we may give up deliberation and choice altogether and lash out destructively at anyone who offends us for any reason at all, real or imagined.

Some angry feelings are minor irritations that flare up in the face of relatively unimportant interactions, are kept to ourselves, and are quickly forgotten. Other angry feelings are reactions to offenses, minor and major, that, when expressed respectfully, can help resolve hurts that otherwise might fester indefinitely. Still other angry feelings are responses to insults and assaults that serve no constructive purpose and that would not happen at all in a more perfect world. These three kinds of angry feelings and the ways we typically express them comprise the range of the "normal" anger that is an inevitable part of ordinary living. All of us deal with such anger on a fairly regular basis.

Not so normal feelings and expressions of anger begin with the grudge harboring that gradually turns life into chronic complaining and looking only for the worst in others. The range widens into the downright "abnormal" feelings of fury, rage, wrath, and hate. Fury, rage, and hate are abnormal in two senses of the word. First, they are exhibited relatively rarely in people whom we consider to be mature and healthy. Second, they run counter to God's loving purpose for all of us. Wrath illustrates this latter consideration especially clearly: seeking vengeance is a matter for God and God alone.

An understanding of what anger is, in all its complexity, is necessary to help us express sufficient empathy toward people in the throes of the deeper and more abiding kinds of anger to which the human spirit is vulnerable. Deeply and chronically angry people are difficult to be around. Understanding them makes it easier to care about and for them. As we will see, empathy also depends on our understanding how and why people get angry in the ways that they do. It is through understanding the what, how, and why of anger, together, that we become best equipped to help ourselves and others work through the many kinds of anger with which we all struggle.

3 Is There a "Christian" Face of Anger?

MANY CHRISTIANS STRUGGLE CONSTANTLY WITH QUESTIONS about anger. For instance, if we grant that people get angry about all kinds of things and that they show their anger in all sorts of ways, is there any reason why Christian men and women should become angry? In other words, aren't we Christians supposed to show the world a better way to live by, among other things, never getting mad?

WHO SAYS WE HAVE TO BE ANGRY?

Several years ago, a couple whom I greatly admire and fondly remember unknowingly forced me to consider anew several of my most cherished convictions about feelings and about how to deal with them. I will refer to the couple by the names Don and Frances (not their own). The conversation that I so well remember took place unexpectedly, in a festive setting.

A large hall was filled with well-wishers, all hoping to express personal greetings to the couple, whose loving family members were enthusiastically helping them celebrate their fiftieth wedding anniversary. Toward the end of the festivities, I finally got the chance I was hoping for to talk briefly with Don and Frances separately. "What do you think has helped the most

*to keep you in love with each other for all these years?" I
asked. Each spouse, out of the other's earshot, told me essentially the same thing: "We learned early on that it's always better to let the sun go down on our anger." Apparently, both did
the same sorts of things not to let show the anger that they
sometimes felt. When Frances knew she was getting miffed,
she headed for her garden in the backyard. Don took his
angry feelings with him to the woodshop in the garage. By
prior agreement, after each calmed down, they would meet on
the porch to say some kind word to each other.*

I have thought many times about this couple's response to me. At
the time, it contradicted almost everything that I thought I knew as a
pastoral counselor about helping people whose anger threatened to
get the better of them. The prevailing doctrine of the mental health
professions on the subject, then and now, can be expressed in many
ways, but all the formulations come to the same thing:

Don't let the sun go down on your anger!
If you keep on holding your anger in, you'll suffer for it.
Tell him how you really feel about the hurt he's caused!
If you've got a gripe, let her have it, straight on.
*There's nothing wrong with a good fight, as long as you
fight fairly.*
It's always better to get the anger out, and the sooner the better.

Several weeks after the celebration, I was visiting in the home of
one of this couple's daughters, whom I will call Beth. In our conversation, we shared our delight over how much everyone enjoyed the
party and over how much her parents meant to all of us. Beth was
curious about the animated chatting she had seen going on between
them and myself. When I told her about it, she laughed heartily and
said: *That's Mom and Dad all right! There's no one in the world who
would ever be able to get them to fight with each other!* When I told
her that I couldn't imagine how they might react to some of the things
I learned about anger from my therapist colleagues, Beth replied:
*They'd probably be confused. The one thing they said to us all the
time when we kids were arguing back and forth was, "Didn't Jesus
tell us not to get angry with each other?"*

A good question! Don and Frances, and many other parents besides, whether Christian or not, take special pains that their children not overlook what the question implies. They do so out of the belief that people can avoid a lot of unpleasantness by trying to live an affirmative answer to it. This belief possesses some truth. Many faces of anger are faces from which we both want to and actually do turn away. By doing so, we can spare ourselves discomfort and, perhaps, even physical harm.

The problem is that most of the faces of anger are unavoidable. The situations that typically provoke anger in human beings are situations that all of us find ourselves in at one time or another, whether they materialize in a grocery store checkout line, a sporting event, a roadway passing lane, the workplace, a schoolroom, a hospital waiting room, around the dining room table, or wherever. These situations and the capacity to become angry, which all human beings share, make it inevitable that all of us, at one time or another, will feel angry at something or somebody. Further, the combination of frustrating situations with our sensitivity to them means that all of us will find ourselves not just with angry feelings but sometimes in a state of anger that does not dissipate easily. Both the feeling and the state can provoke behaviors from us that are either offensive or harmful or both.

The last observation raises for some Christians another interesting faith question. Might it not have been better had God endowed the world either with creatures who are incapable of feeling anger at all or with creatures who at the very least are able to keep their angry feelings under control at all times? The intense discomfort that many people have with anger of any kind, along with the obvious destructive power that resides in the human spirit generally, can make anyone yearn for a world wholly devoid of anger. In fact, is it not just such a world that most of us think heaven will be like? Is there anything wrong with yearning and praying for such a heaven on earth?

As provocative as the possibility might be of a world without anger, our faith tradition provides no answer to the question of why we were not given such a world as a permanent endowment. To my knowledge, Don and Frances never wondered about the possibility.

For them, it was enough to deal with the more practical question of how they should handle the anger that they did in fact feel from time to time, whatever the purpose anger in general might serve in God's overall plan. Not every Christian, however, will find it as easy as Don and Frances did to stay completely away from the kind of faith questions we have just posed. Indeed, one of our own loved ones may be anguishing over them right now, as we might be ourselves. The questions we have been raising are important questions because they go to the heart of our capacity to empathize with people in their angriest moments.

If everybody would be better off if none of us ever got angry, how can it be a good thing to communicate positive regard for someone who consistently lets anger get the better of him or her? Instead of glossing over angry feelings and angry states that may not be good for anybody, should we not be encouraging people to work harder at exorcising their anger altogether? Certainly, Don and Frances are not the only Christians who believe so, but are they right in invoking Jesus' teachings to support their particular approach to dealing with anger? These questions are the subject of the next section.

WHAT DID JESUS SAY ABOUT ANGER?

In Matthew's rendering of Jesus' Sermon on the Mount, our Lord has some startling things to say—both to his audience and to us—about anger, fury, rage, indignation, wrath, and hate. Matthew presents the sayings about anger against the backdrop of Jesus' drawing a sharp contrast between his own teaching and those of the so-called righteous people of his time: "Ye have heard that it was said by them of old time, . . . But I say unto you. . . . " In specific, Jesus' teaching about anger occurs as a comment on the prohibition against killing in Jewish law:

> Ye have heard that it was said by them of old time, Thou shalt not kill; and whosoever shall kill shall be in danger of the judgment: But I say unto you, That whosoever is angry with his brother without a cause shall be in danger of the judgment. (Matthew 5:21-22, KJV)

Jesus' qualification is noteworthy. His condemnation is not of our being angry but of our being angry for no reason. The Revised English Bible renders Jesus' point by means of a very familiar image:

You have heard that our forefathers were told, "Do not commit murder; anyone who commits murder must be brought to justice." But what I tell you is this: Anyone who nurses anger against his brother must be brought to justice.

When we are angry without cause, the anger itself is the primary interest, not the object of our anger and not the anger's satisfactory resolution. "Nursing" anger is a fetching way to render Jesus' point. Good nursing is tending to the needs of the ill, wounded, infirm, and devastated. Nursing our feelings of anger, fury, rage, wrath, indignation, and hate is another matter; it does not promote health. Instead, when we lose sight of what our anger originally was all about, when we nurse our anger, we hold close to our bosom a sense of offense or outrage that cannot possibly be good for us.

As Matthew makes plain in this passage, Jesus' point is not to call into question anything about the ancient prohibition against the *act* of killing. What he invites us to concentrate on, instead, is the feeling of anger in our hearts that can lead someone to kill. It is precisely this kind of anger that can also provoke us to demean people, to let others' indebtedness to us compromise the quality of our relationship with them, and to savor adversarial relationships for their own sake, at the expense of genuine brotherhood and sisterhood.

In the light of this passage from Matthew's Gospel, what can we say about our long-married couple's attitude toward anger? Most importantly, they may have missed some opportunities to discuss between themselves what they did and did not have a right to be angry about. Now, surely, none of us would have been so thoughtless as to say anything like this to Don and Frances in the midst of their celebration. However, we do have the right—and the responsibility—to think the matter through for ourselves, with the help of our Lord's guidance. One thing that leaps from the text is that God expects us to weigh carefully our anger in order to be sure that it is related to some clear cause and not stored up and savored as an end in itself. Jesus does not tell us to get rid of all our anger, period. Instead, he tells us that we are in serious spiritual difficulty when, to change the image slightly, we "suckle" it, for suckling our anger only makes it grow stronger.

The more I listened to Don and Frances talk about how they made their marriage work, the more certain I became that they understood at a very deep level what Jesus was getting at regarding anger. Neither spouse said anything to me that remotely resembled a denial that they ever got angry at all. Rather, they acknowledged—with twinkles in their eyes and good humor in their voices—that sometimes they did get really mad at each other. When they did, they went to their special places to cool down by asking themselves how much the issue between them really mattered. The consistent result, each said, was reassurance that it is only the little things that got them "carrying on" and that none of these things was worth "fussing" about. From Jesus' way of looking at it, Don and Frances did everything within their power *not* to nurse their anger.

As I continue to think about and cherish my brief chats with these wonderful people, I know that there are many who wonder just how many couples like them are left in our fragmented, deeply conflicted, pleasure-seeking society. When I told one therapist colleague some time ago about my experience at the anniversary celebration, his immediate response was, *Are these people for real?* His preliminary judgment was that what made it possible for Don and Frances to set aside anger and to let go of irritability so easily was only an inherent compatibility of personalities that is impossible to reproduce on a wide scale.

Much more was involved than this, however, throughout this couple's entire married life together. Most tellingly, both spouses constantly held up to themselves a clear picture of the kind of people they believed God wanted them to be toward each other. The picture took precedence over anything and everything that they might otherwise have demanded from one other and from their marriage. When Don and Frances retreated to their quiet spots, they brought this picture into view vividly, to shape themselves more fully into its image. They described the process as trying to keep God at the center of their marriage. Many couples today, whatever the degree of compatibility and incompatibility between their personalities, are striving to do the same thing. They, too, are very much "for real," and their successes are neither accidental nor rare.

I did not have a further opportunity to talk with Don and Frances about the deep faith that so obviously informed their commitment to put God first in their marriage. Both are recently deceased. Whether they would have expressed themselves in the language I have just used, we can never know. What they did say about themselves, however, suggests that the wider outlook we are about to consider could not have been far from their own.

ANGER IN BIBLICAL PERSPECTIVE

When Jesus told a crowd of people on the mountain not to hold on to anger without good reason, he was drawing out the implications of a perspective on the whole of human existence in the world, the perspective that informed his existence as a faithful Jew throughout his all-too-short life. Though he spoke specifically about anger, Jesus conveyed the heart of what Judaism believed most deeply about God and about the image of God in each of us. Why are we to take the approach he defined for us toward our anger? Because our very nature, as bearers of God's image, demands that we do so. One passage from the Old Testament expresses this point so powerfully that it is worth our reading it in three translations:

> The LORD is merciful and gracious, slow to anger, and plenteous in mercy. He will not always chide: neither will he keep his anger for ever. He hath not dealt with us after our sins; nor rewarded us according to our iniquities. (Psalm 103:8-10, KJV)

> The LORD is compassionate and gracious,
> long-suffering and ever faithful;
> he will not always accuse
> or nurse his anger for ever.
> He has not treated us as our sins deserve
> or repaid us according to our misdeeds.
> —REB

> Yahweh is tender and compassionate,
> slow to anger, most loving;
> his indignation does not last for ever,
> his resentment exists a short time only;
> he never treats us, never punishes us,
> as our guilt and our sins deserve.
> —JB

As much as we might wish it to be otherwise, however, the Old Testament is also filled with disturbing stories of human behavior at its worst, presided over by a demanding and vengeful God, who inflicts untold harm and misery upon human beings, playing off one individual or group against another for purposes that remain obscure at best and dubious at worst. All of the hostility, mean-spiritedness, and hatefulness that we see in human history is reflected many times over in some of our most widely read Old Testament depictions of God's personhood. We do not have to dwell for very long on the dark side of God that is so evident in the Old Testament to begin wondering, as many Christians did by the second century, how *this* God could possibly be the God and Father of Jesus Christ. Some of these Christians were even speculating that the true God must be another being altogether, inhabiting a realm far above that of the Creator God of the Old Testament.

Providentially, this strange view of God did not prevail in the Christian tradition. The primary reason is that the picture of an unfathomable, threatening, vindictive God is not the predominant picture of God in either the Old or the New Testament. The predominant picture is of a *loving* God. In the Old Testament, specifically, the final word about God's fundamental character is a word that our Lord understood fully: in the mysterious fullness of God's being, divine wrath is swallowed up in divine love: "Plenteous in mercy . . . He hath not . . . rewarded us according to our iniquities."

As it is in God, Jesus says to all who would follow him, so it should be in us. We must reach out to love and serve others, whatever anger, fury, rage, indignation, wrath, and hate we may feel toward them. Consider the following texts, also from the Old Testament:

> *Cease from anger, and forsake wrath: fret not thyself in any wise to do evil. (Psalm 37:8, KJV)*

> *Enough of anger, leave rage aside,*
> *do not worry, nothing but evil can come of it.*
> —*JB*

> *He that is slow to anger is better than the mighty; and he that ruleth his spirit than he that taketh a city. (Proverbs 16:32, KJV)*

> *Better be slow to anger than a fighter,*
> *better control one's temper than capture a city.*
> —*REB*

Three things about these texts, when we consider them together, are especially striking. First, God gets angry, just as we do. Most Christians are very clear about this. Not every Christian, however, is as clear about the second and the third elements in these texts. Second, unlike us, God does not stay angry for very long. Third, God's way of dealing with anger should be our way. In other words: As God's anger is for good cause only, so should ours be. As God's anger is of short duration, so should ours be. As God does not nurse anger, neither should we. As God is gracious and compassionate, so must we be. As Jesus understood all that his tradition said about God in the light of these absolutely primary affirmations, so should we.

However much we emphasize God's gracious love, compassion, patience, and long-suffering, though, we cannot finally avoid the Scriptures' many references to divine anger. God *does* become angry. God's anger is formidable. God would be less than righteous if God were never to become angry. And a lot of God's anger is with *us*. We can never hope to experience the fullness of God's mercy unless and until we acknowledge these basic truths about our creaturely existence and about our relationship with our Creator.

Having acknowledged this much, we also must pay heed to something in the Scriptures that is of greater importance still: the constant reminder that high as the heavens are above the earth are God's ways above our ways. This truth applies especially powerfully to the feeling of anger. Though not of an order altogether other than our own, God's anger, nevertheless, is quite different from most of the anger that we feel and exhibit on most occasions. As Jesus expressed it, the Father's anger is *for cause*. It is anger that God has a right and a reason to feel; it is anger with a purpose. By contrast, most of our anger—finite, fallible, self-centered, sinful creatures that we are—is all out of proportion to its provocations, self-serving, and prolonged more for its own sake than for anything good that we might ever bring out of it.

THE PURPOSE OF GOD'S ANGER

In God's anger are cause and purpose, which are often conspicuously lacking in our own. How might we understand this about God? What does God have a right and a reason to be angry about? In a word, us. We have strayed from God's ways like lost sheep. Even now, God calls us into a special relationship to tend the creation lovingly, to reconcile humankind's warring families and nations by showing them the better way of loving God and all our neighbors as we love ourselves, glorifying God's only Son in all that we do. And yet, as our fathers, mothers, brothers, and sisters in all generations have done, we put ourselves first, ignoring and even denying our Creator's will and hopes for us, spewing out our anger onto anyone and everyone we perceive to be obstacles to our own pursuits in a world that we have falsely come to believe is there for our taking.

As the Scriptures tell us repeatedly, all of us have sinned and fallen short of the glory of God. And we continue to do so. Is it any wonder, then, that our Creator becomes angry at times? Does God not have "cause" to be? In light of the precarious position we constantly put ourselves in by persistent indifference and even hostility toward God's plan for the world, how could God not be angry?

But what specifically is God's anger like? Has God revealed enough of the divine self in the Scriptures to give us a picture sufficiently clear to use as a model for dealing with our own anger? For Christians, the answer to this question is a resounding yes. Bringing what we need to answer the question into view, however, requires that we consider specific texts on the subject only in the light of what the biblical witness as a whole tells us about God. We are not to fixate on one text or cluster of texts that happens at the moment to serve our own purposes.

Some people, for instance, picture God's anger as a world-destroying fury whose effects are like firestorms generated by volcanic eruptions. The treatment of Sodom and Gomorrah in Genesis 19 is but one example. Texts like this one are made to stand for everything that the Bible has to say about anger in God. Even today, in spite of what the Book of Genesis also says about God's covenant with Noah—never again to inflict destruction on the whole of creation—some continue to hurl predictions at us of our catastrophic end at the hands of an out-of-patience Creator.

Others see God's anger manifesting itself in more measured ways, for instance, in scenarios of punishment meted out by antagonists who may or may not have any real conception of the part they are playing in the grand scheme of divine justice—the Assyrians, Babylonians, and Romans, to name some of the better known. And still others, serious students of the Book of Job, for example, struggle with the possibility that God's anger may be merely sadistic in nature, inflicting pain and suffering for reasons that remain swallowed up in impenetrable mystery. The elder brother in Luke's parable of the prodigal son seems also to have a keen understanding of what being out of favor with God, unjustly, is all about.

That such pictures have a basis in scriptural texts is beyond dispute. But do they reflect accurately the biblical message as a whole? They do not if the passages we looked at earlier are any indication. In those passages, God is pictured as slow to anger, as angry for short durations only, as conveying compassion far more than anger, and as withholding rather than invoking punishments that we deserve to receive.

Some of the anger that God displays seems rather clearly rooted in disappointment. God feels disappointment that we do not acknowledge with gratitude the divine gifts of life, fellowship, calling, and purpose. The Lord feels disappointment that we so often fail to live up both to the Lord's expectations of us and our own expectations of ourselves. And God feels disappointment that the divine vision for the whole of things must remain frustrated until we finally claim the freedom with which God has endowed us to participate with "gladsome hearts" in bringing about the kind of joyful future God intends for us.

Not all of the anger that God reveals has disappointment as its foundation. Some anger seems equally to be rooted in God's sense of being betrayed by us. From the time of Adam's exhilarated sigh of relief over receiving a suitable helper until the present day, the pattern is the same: with our lips we extol our Creator's graciousness and then promptly set about doing things our way rather than God's way, tasting forbidden fruits of all kinds, seizing lands not intended for us, delighting in liberation but rejecting its hardships, worshiping idols, setting our own makeshift kingdoms above the permanence and glory of God's, denying Christ time and time again—and on and on.

Our broken promises to God strew the sacred spaces in which we seek the divine presence without worship, blessings without responsibilities, and gifts without service. Still, we go on promising. And by continuing to let our promises matter, fully aware that we are far more likely to break than to honor them, God makes the divine self vulnerable to the kind of anger that anyone who bears the divine image must feel when hope and trust are dashed. It is possible, of course, to envision a God whose own supreme otherness makes the Deity utterly impervious to anything that we might do or not do. Indeed, many philosophers and theologians have argued that only this kind of being is properly called God. The Scriptures make plain, however, that whatever else might be said of such a being, we cannot call this one the Father of Abraham, of Isaac, of Jacob, and of our Lord Jesus Christ. The Father of our Lord cares enough for the divine creation to become angry about things that take place in it.

Deeper than disappointment and a sense of betrayal, however, is the purposive nature of God's anger. Just as there is reason for it, there is purpose served by it. What is this purpose? Most basically, it is to capture our attention so that we may focus again on what God asks of us as creatures with the mission to represent the Deity in the world. The sense of having displeased our Creator, when heeded, can reawaken us to our true identity and purpose, not merely to avoid "getting what is coming to us," but rather to reclaim our proper dignity as God's faithful servants. God's displeasure with us serves the primary purpose of making us displeased with what we are making of ourselves and desirous all over again of becoming what God wants to make of us. When God's anger accomplishes that purpose, the Deity has no need to nurse it further. This is why, with the psalmist, we can rejoice that God's anger (unlike ours) exists a short time only and that, ultimately, what we see on God's face is not anger but mercy.

SUMMARY

We close this chapter with a brief summary, applying a biblical perspective on anger to answering the question with which this chapter is titled. Is there a "Christian" face of anger? Or, as Don and Frances might have asked the question, Is it really all right for a Christian to be angry?

The fundamental principle for faith contained in the Scriptures is that God calls us to express our anger in the way that God expresses divine anger. Since God does not stifle anger, God does not demand that we stifle ours. Indeed, from the standpoint of our faith, the capacity to feel anger is part of our very nature as created beings, one of our Creator's most precious gifts to us. But God does not store up anger, nursing it so that it takes on a life of its own. God feels and expresses anger only when circumstances warrant doing so and then moves on. Allowing the created order to matter enough that God is significantly affected by the events that transpire in it, God makes the divine self vulnerable to the disappointments and betrayals that provoke divine anger in the first place. Then, God uses divine anger to motivate us when we offend, to recapture a lively sense of who we are in God's sight and of what God asks from us as those who bear the divine image in the world.

The single most important lesson to be drawn from this chapter is this: the fury, rage, and retaliation that are so much a part of our own angry reactions have no place in God. Our offenses toward God never overwhelm divine compassion, patience, grace, and love. As God treats us, so are we to treat all whom God loves.

4 How and Why We Get Angry

THE FIRST THREE CHAPTERS OF THIS BOOK HAVE BEEN DEVOTED TO characterizing what anger is as a cluster of feelings and expressions of feelings. We now turn our attention to the process of anger, to describing what goes on in and between us whenever we become angry, whether we keep within ourselves or express openly what we are feeling. Two fundamental convictions guide the discussion. First, a common origin underlies all the shapes that anger may assume on particular occasions—from barely noticeable irritation all the way to torrid hate. Moreover, what underlies every feeling of anger influences the entire process of our becoming angry in the first place and of our deciding how to express, or not express, the anger we feel. Second, every feeling and expression of anger is made possible by the same divine gift of the very capacity to feel anger at all. How we can learn to be grateful for this precious gift, in spite of the myriad ways our uses of it defy its Giver's intent, is the single most important concern of this chapter.

ANGER STARTS EARLY

Sometimes, the reaction comes out all by itself. At other times, a gentle slap is necessary to provoke it. In both cases, the sound is familiar:

the first cry of a startled newborn. The cry expresses both displeasure and demand, mobilizing caregivers for swift, remedial action. If the response fails to alleviate the frustration, or if it is simply tardy, the results are thoroughly predictable: more crying! This time, though, the crying will be more insistent, in proportion to the need's urgency. From the beginning, infants tell us important things about themselves and about what they need from us. Their cries and howls contain messages that even the most fatigued, self-doubting caregivers cannot miss.

What gives intensity to infants' cries is their helplessness to meet their own needs and their dependence upon us to supply them instead. Given their extreme vulnerability, infants simply must get our attention. However, even the most competent nurturers, committed to anticipating as many of their charges' needs as possible, sometimes require the kind of reminding that only an unholy squalling can accomplish. Providentially, infants come into the world equipped by our Creator to make their needs known to us quickly and relentlessly.

From our earliest moments outside our mothers' wombs, our getting angry is indispensable to getting our most basic needs met. We might put the operative principle this way: *Don't stay needy; get really mad!* Infants rarely abuse this principle. A cry almost always indicates a need. With adults, however, the situation is often different.

BUT ANGER DOESN'T COME FIRST

One of the most important things that mental health professionals have to teach us about anger is its identification as a *secondary,* rather than *primary,* feeling. That is, we feel angry after we have felt something else first—a fact that is easy to overlook. Whenever anger is present, whether in ourselves or in someone nearby, it usually claims the center stage of our attention. If the anger is our own, we often act as if its alleviation is absolutely necessary to our getting on with anything else; for example: *I can't be bothered with anything else right now; I'm going to go over there and give him a piece of my mind.* Or: *I'm so angry with her that all I can think about is what she did to me.* If it is someone else who is angry, we may find ourselves caught up in an angry reaction to the anger itself; for example: *It's three in the morning; can't you get that kid to shut up?* Or: *Don't you ever speak to me in that tone of voice again.*

As prominent as anger is whenever it makes its appearance, it is nevertheless and always a reaction to something else that we are feeling, and its primary purpose is to draw our attention to that "something else." To put the point another way, anger is always *about* something else. Therefore, if we or others around us become angry, it is both appropriate and necessary to ask: *What is it that I am really so angry about? What is it that you are really so angry about?* Until we know the answers to these questions, we cannot get to the heart of the anger, and we will remain impaired in our ability to do much that is constructive about it.

Anger, displayed from earliest infancy throughout life, is most essentially the natural expression of feelings of deprivation. Deprived of something basic to our existence—for example, security, nourishment, a loving presence—and feeling the deprivation, we are, by the grace of God, equipped to set up a fuss and, if necessary, even a riot in order to gain relief. When babies are satisfied, anger dissipates quickly, to the gratitude of worn-out parents and nurturers everywhere.

The relationship between perceiving deprivation and reacting with anger, forged in the crucible of our earliest experiences, is a relationship that continues throughout our lives. No matter how mature we become, we will go on reacting to feelings of deprivation with anger and needing the alleviation of both the anger and the deprivation. However, important differences exist between the dynamics of anger in infancy and in adulthood. Confusing or discounting these differences is the major source of most of our failures as adults to deal with anger constructively.

SOONER OR LATER, WE HAVE TO GROW UP

Normally, we do not expect infants to do anything about their anger other than to bring it to full expression. It is our job, not the infant's, to take it from there. Sometimes, we might wish it to be otherwise—for example, if our baby's colic runs into a fifth or sixth month. However, when we regather our wits about us, we remember that the baby's protracted fussiness and fits are for a reason, even when we are desperate for them to stop. Difficult as it can be to satisfy an out-of-sorts infant, we nevertheless bear the responsibility to keep on struggling until we discover something that meets the need at least some of the time.

Though demanding in practice, the process of caring for angry infants is quite easy to understand: they need, they demand, we relieve. The process of getting angry is little different for adults than it is for infants: in both, anger stems from felt deprivation and the anxiety that accompanies it, anxiety over whether our needs will be met by whomever. Further, for both infants and adults the purpose of becoming angry in the midst of frustration is the same: our anger calls attention to a need that warrants a response. At this point, however, the resemblance between infants' and adults' experiences of anger diminishes considerably.

Unlike infants, adults develop wants in addition to needs and can become just as angry about a frustrated preference as about an unmet need. For the purposes of the present discussion, a *want* is an attraction to something we may believe will enhance our lives but which, in fact, is not essential either to our survival or our well-being. By contrast, a *need* is a craving for what is absolutely necessary to our becoming what our Creator intends for us to become. On a list of wants, which is almost infinitely expandable in a consumer-oriented society, we might include things that range all the way from self-repairing appliances, bigger cars, faster modems, diets that work, and risk-free sex, to conflict-free relationships, permanent employment, a climate-controlled environment, and world domination. Our list of needs will be considerably shorter: for example, food, clothing, safety, love, meaning. Part of what it means to be a mature adult is the ability to distinguish being angry over not getting something that we need from being angry over not getting something that we want.

A second major difference between infants and adults surfaces when it comes to meeting one's own needs. While infants are incapable of getting any of their anger-provoking needs met all by themselves, adults can meet at least some of theirs. Further, adults are rightly expected to meet as many of them as they can. Not all adults find this expectation to their liking. Some steadfastly refuse to modify the dependent style that they found acceptable in infancy and choose instead to act like petulant children all their lives, angrily blaming others for whatever frustrations and dissatisfactions they constantly bring upon themselves. More mature adults use the messages contained in their angry feelings to do whatever they can on their own to make things better for themselves.

Yet another difference between infants and adults emerges with regard to manifestations of anger. While the anger of infants immediately turns into protest and demand, the anger of adults is expected to lead to self-reflection, deliberation, and request. As our capacities for self-knowledge, independent judgment, and decision making grow, so does our responsibility for being aware of our frustrations and for discovering the most effective means of alleviating them, requesting but not demanding others' involvement when we see that we cannot do it all on our own. While infants have no choice but to lay upon others the responsibility for satisfying their needs, adults decide whether to remain children in this respect or to aim toward both self-sufficiency and attentiveness to the needs of others. For those who choose the latter course, a healthy and fulfilling interdependence is the reward, reciprocal relationships in which each partner is of help to the other, ungrudgingly and lovingly.

BEING ANGRY FOR GOOD REASON AND FOR NO REASON

To this point in the chapter, we have focused on the feeling of anger as a reaction to felt deprivation. Contained in this statement is a distinction between an actual state (of really being deprived of something important) and the awareness of that state (as manifested in hunger, thirst, cold, fear, loneliness, etc.). This distinction is important enough to warrant a closer look. It implies, first, that we can actually be undergoing deprivation without being aware of it at the time. For instance, if we are busily engaged in work or play outdoors on a hot summer day, we may be on the verge of dehydration well before we realize how thirsty we have become. Or if it falls to us to make all of the burial arrangements for a favorite family member, it may be some time before we acknowledge how deeply sad we ourselves are. With respect to feelings of anger, even though we may be going through very real deprivation, unless we feel that deprivation, we do not get angry about it.

The distinction between deprivation suffered and deprivation felt implies that we can feel deprived and be angry about it even when we are not deprived. For example, even though we are well nourished by a splendidly prepared evening meal, we attempt to raid the refrigerator later and grumble at the sight of its empty shelves. Or even though we receive good raises and early promotions at work, we complain about being overworked and underappreciated. As these examples illustrate, we can feel deprivation when there is none and, as a consequence, be angry for no reason. The single most important implication of the distinction between actual and acknowledged deprivation is this: we have the right to feel anger and to have our feeling taken seriously when (and only when) our anger relates to a real deprivation. In the absence of such a deprivation, our anger degenerates into mere pouting and griping that both we and those around us are better off without.

To some, this last statement may seem harsh. After all, are not all feelings involuntary reactions that are neither good nor bad, praiseworthy nor blameworthy, in themselves? Should we not therefore reserve our applause and our criticism for what we *do* and not for what we *feel*? Isn't being empathic largely a matter of encouraging and receiving expressions of feelings without judgment of any kind? To a great extent, the answer to all these questions is a clear yes. We cannot help the way we feel a lot of the time; in the long run, our actions do count for more than either our words or our feelings; and loving family members and friends listen well for all kinds of feelings, making no assumptions in advance about which should be honored and which should be disparaged. Having acknowledged this much, however, we still are on solid ground maintaining that the distinction between real and felt deprivation leads straightaway to the conclusion that some anger is justified, that is, "for cause," and some is not.

ANGER IS MORE THAN A FEELING

Thus far, we have answered the "why" question about our anger by exploring the connections between feeling angry and feeling deprived: we get angry because we are in need and for the purpose of attracting the attention of those who can help us satisfy that need. Much of what we have discovered about the why of anger also sheds light on the process of becoming angry in the first place and of acknowledging and dealing with anger once it is aroused in us. We have described this process in terms of felt deprivation, whether anchored in actual deprivation or not, triggering feelings of anger and mobilizing efforts to relieve frustration(s). Two things impede the last stage of this process.

The first impediment to resolving our anger satisfactorily is our unwillingness to give up our childhood fantasy that the alleviation of frustration is always someone else's responsibility. Refusal to give up the fantasy is refusal to grow up. It is to decide for holding on to very primitive patterns of voicing angry feelings indiscriminately, to all and sundry, with no regard for how our doing so might affect anyone else. The second impediment has to do with the activation of one or more assumptions, convictions, and even doctrines about how things should go in life and about what deprivations we should and should not be expected to endure. Clues to the existence and power of these kinds of beliefs are contained in statements such as

Nobody should have to go through what you are going through.

This should never have happened.

I deserve better.

They can't let this go on much longer.

Everything eventually works out for the best.

If our philosophy of life includes beliefs like these, then our anger is likely to be even stronger when a particular felt deprivation runs counter to one or more of them. What this means is that anger is not only a matter of what we feel; it is also a matter of what we do and do not believe about the world. That is, it is conditioned by both our feelings of deprivation and our beliefs. Holding on to certain sorts of beliefs will make it inevitable that, given some frustration or other, we will get angry, perhaps intensely angry, and stay angry for a long time. Holding to other sorts of beliefs, on the other hand, may make it possible for us to endure very serious deprivations for extended periods of time and feel little or no anger at all.

By way of illustration, several years ago I had occasion to visit with two men whose jobs had been terminated as a part of their company's downsizing. The reactions of the two men, whom I will call Sam and Will, are summarized in the following statements:

Sam: *Who do those bean counters think they are, doing this to a guy like me, who's worked his heart out for this company? Year after year, taking whatever they threw at me, never complaining, always available. I don't deserve this! It's not fair! You better believe they're gonna pay for this.*

Will: *At first it was pretty much of a shock to hear that I didn't have a job anymore. And for a couple of days, I guess, I thought about getting a real mad on about it. But, you know, loyalty is a thing of the past, and business does this kind of thing all the time now. I really don't have any right to expect that I'd be spared when others aren't. So, I'm putting it behind me and concentrating on what's next.*

Sam and Will are suffering the same genuine deprivation: the unexpected loss of their means of livelihood. Their reactions to the deprivation, though, are anything but the same.

Sam is caught up in anger so intense that it threatens to undermine his getting back into the workforce quickly, or even at all. By contrast, Will is almost serene in his acceptance of the situation; whatever anger he may have felt initially seems to have dissipated almost completely. What contributes so powerfully to Sam's anger is the strong conviction that he clings to about how things are supposed to go in the world of work: if we are loyal to our employers, our employers will be loyal to us. Will holds to a quite different belief: business is business, and no employment carries permanent guarantees. His conspicuous absence of anger is made possible largely by the congruence between what he believes happens in business generally and what has in fact happened in his own case. Had he believed what Sam believes, he might be as angry as Sam is.

Another illustration comes from an all-too-frequent experience nowadays: encounters with angry drivers. Sometimes, we may even be the angry drivers ourselves! What lies behind any form of road rage is the same thing that lies behind every other feeling of anger: a feeling of deprivation. Angry drivers are angry, in part, because they feel frustrated over not being able to achieve something that is important to them at the moment—for example, getting to a meeting on time, beating rush-hour traffic home, enjoying a meandering drive through the country without being honked at from behind, and so on. Sometimes drivers take out their frustrations over things that have nothing to do with what other drivers may be doing at the time. In either case, however, felt frustration is only part of the anger.

The more important element is what enraged drivers believe, usually without being aware of it or without being willing to admit it, about what should and should not be happening to them on the road. Invariably, their beliefs contain the same two elements: an assertion of special privilege and an insistence that their frustration is someone else's fault. For example:

My time and agenda are more important than anyone else's time and agenda.

Other drivers should know of my special needs and accommodate them.

When there is not enough room for both others and me on the road, the others should get off and let me through.

Others' insensitivity to me and my situation is the source of all my frustrations.

For reasonable people, beliefs like these are both preposterous and dangerous. Considering even the possibility that we might harbor any of them should provoke more than just a mild sense of horror. Nevertheless, even the most reasonable among us act on occasion as if we believed such things. Because this is so, unless we constantly subject these absurd beliefs to appropriate criticism, we will remain vulnerable to the very kind of enraged reactions that we so deplore in others.

Anger arises in us when feelings of deprivation interact with beliefs that we hold about how things should and should not go in our lives. Relating the feelings to real, instead of to imagined, deprivation, along with subjecting our beliefs to careful evaluation and changing them as the evaluation warrants, will help us to deal constructively not only with our anger but also with the frustrations that give rise to it. For some, however, all this is more easily said than done.

TOO MANY DEPRIVATIONS, TOO MUCH ANGER

From the perspective of the Christian faith, we can and should do a great deal to bring our angry feelings under the sway of careful deliberation and responsible action. In the process, we are to respect anger that is "for cause" and put aside anger that is not. Just as God has endowed us with the capacity to feel anger and to react angrily when real deprivations demand, the Almighty has given us powers of discrimination and judgment and expects us to use these powers in a manner befitting our nature as creatures bearing God's own image.

By contrast, modern psychology tends to see feelings as exempted from moral evaluation altogether. Feelings are neither good nor bad, responsible nor irresponsible, in themselves; they just are. Instead of stifling feelings by concerns about obligation, responsibility, and duty, we are to raise these latter concerns only in reference to the actions that our feelings influence. Though it is both proper and necessary to determine what we should and should not do, applying "should" and "should not" to what we feel is never proper and always destructive. By way of example, modern psychology views statements like *You shouldn't be feeling that way* as never justifiable. According to this point of view, holding people accountable for their feelings, in addition to their actions, reflects a morally bankrupt kind of judgmentalism that can only harm the human spirit.

On the face of it, some strong differences appear to exist between what our faith and what the mental health professions have to say about the how and the why of feelings; however, these differences, though real, are neither fundamental nor irreconcilable. From a Christian perspective, the truth in psychological approaches to feelings lies in their reminder that sometimes some people have difficulty controlling one or more of their feelings and that at those times others' compassion usually proves more helpful than their criticism. Rather than resting content in affirming only this much about the life of feelings, however, psychology typically races headlong toward the extreme position that all feelings always fall under the sway of involuntary processes over which we have little, if any, control and for which, therefore, we have no real responsibility.

The truth, rather than the excess, in psychology's understanding of anger will prove especially helpful to us in this section as we focus on a form of anger to which we have not as yet paid sufficient attention: cumulative anger that is rooted in massive, unrelieved deprivation over a long period of time. This is the anger of those genuinely and tragically victimized, especially by poverty, multiple losses, chronic illness, harassment, and violence. Some who endure such deprivations are only too aware of how angry they are and of how helpless they are to do anything about what provokes their anger continuously. Others push the remembrance of hunger, loss, sickness, and assaults as far from consciousness as their fragile psyches will allow, only to be intruded upon repeatedly by suddenly awakened memories of only partially forgotten horrors. And still others turn into furious, hateful, and destructive people who frighten and even threaten everyone around them.

From a vantage point of relative comfort and security, we sometimes find it difficult to acknowledge just how much undeserved deprivation so many people on earth continue to suffer. After all, we ask, is it not true that much of the misery that people suffer is misery that they bring upon themselves by their own poor judgments and irresponsible actions? Are not their miseries their "just desserts"? Under these circumstances, do they have any right to be angry about what happens to them?

To some extent, such questions are valid, even if they lack empathy and compassion. It is true that, sometimes, we have only ourselves to blame for bad things happening; our anger about them is, therefore, out of place. For instance, if we build our home on the seashore for the sake of a glorious view, we must consider the possibility of losing it to a violent hurricane. Or if we avoid associating with or offering help to our colleagues at work, we must consider the possibility that they will not be there for us if and when we need them. However, many people do not get what they "deserve" in life, even remotely. True innocents suffer and die from unpredictable natural disasters, malnutrition, painful diseases, and others' indifference, stupidity, and abuse—even as those who deserve all these and more escape from them entirely. Attempts to minimize or explain away such injustices border on obscenity, if not blasphemy.

It should not surprise us that people to whom life deals out more than a fair share of troubles typically carry around a great deal of anger. Even so, the anger of the chronically aggrieved can be awesome in its intensity. Getting over being angry is a manageable task if the anger stems only from the kinds of deprivations, frustrations, and losses with which all of us, by virtue of being human beings in an imperfect world, must deal. For the truly victimized, however, the task can be monumental. Anger from long-standing, deliberately inflicted deprivations accumulates with malignant force over the passage of time. People who are caught up in the resulting and unresolved fury, rage, wrath, or hate may find it pouring out of them at the least provocation, all out of proportion to the specific insult at hand. Bewildered, others may ask, *What could possibly be behind that much anger?*

Nothing in the previous paragraph is intended to suggest that any of us, however victimized, is somehow exempt from having to learn to deal with our anger as our Lord taught us to do. Indeed, on the cross, Jesus himself became the exemplar of how to express the anger that the most demonic assaults spawn: "Father, forgive them; for . . ." (Luke 23:34). From the standpoint of our Christian faith, we cannot be merely neutral about feelings of anger. Some forms of anger, and some of the ways we give them expression, simply run counter to how God desires for us to deal with the created order. In spite of this fundamental fact about our existence in the world, however, all too many people still want only to give free rein to their displeasure, to "let it all hang out," and to blame others for it. Some of these, however, may have less initial choice in the matter than others, even though they may wish it to be otherwise. One person I know put it this way: *I want so much to control my temper better, but I wonder whether I'm ever going to get better at it.*

This plaintive statement was shared with me some years ago by a man in his late twenties who was just beginning the painful process of recalling to mind a childhood shattered by an abusive father and uncle and by a stream of sadistic older men his mother entertained, for fees, well into his high school years. Finally, facing up to what his own uncontrolled outbursts of anger were doing to his marriage, career hopes, and friendships, this young man began the hard work of getting to the bottom of them. It took a while for him to begin feeling more confident about his ability to control and direct his anger. Even then, he shared, *I still feel sometimes that I'm only one provocation away from all my old stuff coming up again.*

Like this conscientious young man, many people suffer extreme vulnerability to towering outbursts of anger because too many horrific things have happened to them for too long. We have no right to suppose that such a state of vulnerability provides any excuse for refusing to deal constructively with the anger that in part it generates. However, respecting the fact that any of us, given the wrong circumstances, can develop such vulnerability may help us to understand and to show compassion toward anyone who may not seem to be managing the task as well as others do.

WHEN OUR WANTS ARE NOT SUPPLIED

Before we bring this chapter to a close, we must deal with one final issue about anger, one that goes to the heart of our faith. Some assume that dealing with anger is easy if we will only bring faith resources to the task. Faith does make a difference, a large and positive difference, in not letting anger get in the way of growing spiritually as God wants us to grow. However, when the problem is one of how to manage our anger, our faith may become more part of the problem than of the solution. What is there in our faith that calls for such a strange-sounding assertion?

A young widow, whom I shall call Ellie, offers an especially poignant answer to this question. Struggling to make ends meet, with no family support, and finding no adequate medical care for a child severely disabled from birth, Ellie is close to the breaking point and cries out to her friend Marge, *God broke his promises to me!* The conversation continued as follows:

Marge: *Would you tell me a little more about those promises, Ellie?*

Ellie: *I've heard all my life that God will always give me what I need, that he'll never give me more than I can handle. Well, I can't get what I need from him or from anybody else, and I sure can't handle what I've got. I'm at the end of my rope, Marge. I'm done in, and I'm done.*

Marge: *You trusted God, and he's let you down. And the pain of it is almost more than you can stand.*

Ellie: *There's no "almost" about it. I can't stand it anymore. Right now I'm so mad at God that I can't see straight.*

Marge: *Ellie, what you just said is what I thought I was hearing before. Your words were telling me that you couldn't go on, but they had more of an angry than a despairing sound to them. Am I hearing you right?*

Ellie: *Yeah, I guess so. I know I have to go on, whether I want to or not. What would happen to my little boy if I just give up? But it doesn't mean I have to like it or to love God anymore. I'm too angry with him to depend on anything I hear about him.*

If life does not improve for Ellie and her son, she will likely fall into the kind of despair that Marge is presently listening for, but not finding, in this conversation. For now, however, Ellie's primary feeling is anger—bitter, unrepentant, righteous anger. One of Ellie's best friends thoroughly rejects her in her present state: *Ellie, how can you even think such a thing about God? You should be ashamed of the way you're feeling.* Marge understands the situation much better. She sees clearly that Ellie's predicament has become even more painful to endure by the very faith that Ellie brings to it. Ellie trusted the things that she was told about God enough to believe them herself. And because she still holds on to these cherished beliefs, she is outraged that they seem completely contradicted by the events of her own life.

One way to characterize what Ellie wants to believe about God is in the language of the familiar hymn by Henry Alford, "Come, Ye Thankful People, Come." Its first verse contains these uplifting words: "God, our Maker, doth provide for our wants to be supplied." Alford's words capture, in the context of giving thanks for a plentiful harvest, the sense of one of the most powerful and moving passages in all of Scripture, the opening verse of the Twenty-third Psalm: "The Lord is my shepherd; I shall not want." Ellie, who has trusted in just such a God, now confronts the searing possibility that God has failed her, and she is overwhelmed with anger about it. Unlike Ellie's other friend, who is eerily reminiscent of some of Job's companions, Marge responds with understanding and compassion: God does seem to have failed Ellie, and Ellie has every right to be angry about it. In words that we have used repeatedly, Ellie's anger seems to be "for cause."

Undeserved abandonment, hardships, and afflictions can erode the faith of even the most committed Christians. Unrelieved, they can hinder our best efforts to trust in God, serving only as painful signs of broken promises. Sometimes, wants are not "supplied," the harvest is anything but plentiful, and spirits, weakened from one disappointment after the other, finally break.

Ellie's burdens are different from those of some frustrated souls who are quick to blame God for every unanticipated interruption in their lives. One person I know took being denied an expected promotion as a sign of God's impotence to be of any help at all in her life. Another railed against God for not making his girlfriend love him more. Both spoke of God's not meeting their "needs." Instead, their friends, myself included, chided them for remaining peevish about not getting what they *want* instead of focusing on what they really *need*. To be sure, wants are important, as is distress over their frustration. If they are deserved, promotions should be forthcoming. And love returned enhances life significantly. Nevertheless, we can and do survive career setbacks and unrequited feelings. With respect to what Ellie wants so desperately, however, further deprivation may lead, at the very least, to an irrecoverable loss of hope. Unlike my two friends, Ellie has earned the right to complain loudly about unmet needs.

The way we now use the words *want* and *need* to distinguish between kinds of desiring and striving is, in general, helpful. We do indeed yearn for what we both can and cannot do without. Our problem is that our faith tradition, transmitted by means of earlier English language usage, refers to needs like Ellie's by the word *wants*. However, the possible confusion is easily sorted out. What we must focus on is the temptation in all of us to treat both wants and needs equally, expecting that both be satisfied on demand. God, however, makes it plain that a life of service demands sacrifices from us, especially of many allurements that we typically want the most and falsely believe that we must have. In return for relinquishing self-absorption in the interest of serving others in God's name, God promises that our own wants, here understood as "needs," will be supplied. This is what Ellie has counted on, whatever words may be used to express it, and this is what she has now come to doubt. Ellie is suffering deprivation not just of things she wants but could do without; her deprivation and suffering are over things that she genuinely and desperately needs.

In this light, we can appreciate just how relieved Marge is to hear Ellie speak the way she does: *Praise God for Ellie's anger! It says that she still has a strong belief in God. Without it, given all that she has to struggle with, Ellie just might go over the edge.* Marge understands correctly that she cannot be of help to Ellie unless she honors Ellie's anger. She also trusts that the very anger that now seems to reflect Ellie's eroding faith can also become a way into deeper trust of God's constant love.

SUMMARY

In this chapter we have looked below the surface of very different feelings and expressions of anger to the underlying process that is common to all of them. Anger begins in deprivation and the feeling of deprivation. Even its most misguided and repugnant expressions have as their overarching purpose the alleviation of some lack, loss, frustration, need, or want. The single most important point of the chapter is that we cannot hope to manage and control anger, especially its more malignant expressions, unless we first acknowledge and respect (1) the ways by which all of us come to feel anger of any kind, and (2) the purposes that all anger seeks to serve.

The relationship between deprivation and anger is complex. We can be in a state of actual deprivation without feeling deprived and therefore fail to experience the anger that we might otherwise. We can feel deprivation when we are not actually deprived and, as a result, become angry without good reason. We can feel both deprived and angry all out of proportion to the real deprivation behind the feelings. And, whatever our anger may be about in one situation or another, we can choose to give it expression in any number of ways, just as we can choose to hold it within ourselves completely. Also affecting our feelings of anger, and the decisions we make about expressing them, are the beliefs we hold about what kinds of frustrations we should and should not have to endure in life.

We can view all feelings and expressions of anger as part of a continuum. Along the continuum, we can identify anger that falls in the range of "normal and everyday" experiences that come and go without troubling us very much and anger that cries out for serious and sustained concern as it becomes increasingly destructive and defies easy control. Understanding the continuum is important to our distinguishing the kinds of anger—in ourselves and others—with which we can deal on our own from those that are likely to require professional help.

That all angry feelings share a common origin does not mean, however, that we should not attempt to distinguish them according to a scale of value. From the standpoint of our faith tradition, a great deal of anger has a *negative* value, serving only hurtful purposes. Some of our angry feelings, according to this same tradition, are *positive* and, as such, are worthy of cultivation and nurture. About some things, we *should* be angry. One of our Christian responsibilities is to learn just what those things are, so that we can gradually learn to be angry "for cause."

5 Dealing with Everyday Anger

UNDERSTANDING THE WHAT, HOW, AND WHY OF ANGER FROM the perspectives of the mental health professions and our faith tradition, the focus of the preceding chapters, is a prerequisite to applying the understanding to our daily lives as Christians, whether as caring family members, friends, fellow citizens, lay shepherds, or pastors. We can apply the understanding to two contexts: to ourselves and to our relationships. The first section of this chapter illustrates how we can use the material discussed thus far for dealing with our own angry feelings. Then, the remaining sections introduce the subject matter for the rest of the book: caring about and for angry people.

Although we examine the contexts as two distinct ones, much about them are inseparable. Just as we are more likely to understand better someone else's anger by looking honestly at our own, we are also more likely to understand better our own anger by paying respectful attention to anger in others. In this regard, this chapter discusses helping people, ourselves included, with what we have previously referred to as the "normal" kinds of anger that are part and parcel of ordinary daily living. The next two chapters, by contrast, direct attention to the darker sides of anger and its expression, with a particular concern to identify the kinds of angry people who need more help than most caring friends and pastors can provide.

HEALING OUR OWN ANGER

One of the most important things the ancient philosopher Socrates learned about life, from an oracle at Delphi, was "Know thyself." The oracle's words are as important for us as they were for Socrates, for surely, if we are to make any contribution at all to reversing the rising tides of anger that threaten to engulf our social order, we must begin with ourselves. We must learn to acknowledge and respect the kinds of anger we typically feel (and do not feel), the circumstances under which we most often become angry, whether and to what extent we express our anger openly, what we most characteristically do in order to get our anger behind us, and whether our usual strategies for dealing with anger are effective.

A good way to examine and assess our angry feelings and how we typically deal with them is through a personal journal in which we record on a regular basis our thoughts on our feelings and expressions of anger. Sometimes, journal keeping goes better when it is guided by questions specifically designed to facilitate self-expression. With regard to focusing on our own anger, the following questions usually prove helpful:

1. How often do I get angry? Not often? Very often? More than I would like? More than others would like?
2. When I am angry, do others typically know it? How?
3. Do I know pretty much in advance what is likely to set me off and what isn't?
4. What sorts of things, if any, (a) irritate me somewhat, (b) get other peoples' backs up but not mine, (c) make me quite angry, (d) almost drive me up the wall or over the edge?
5. Does it seem that the anger I feel on most occasions is about the right amount or intensity depending on what my anger is about at the time? Have there been times when my anger has "bent me out of shape" more than I should have allowed? If so, how and why might I have let it happen? If not, what do I typically do to curtail it?

6. What, for me, are (*a*) acceptable and (*b*) unacceptable ways of expressing anger? Do I expect other people to live up to these same standards? Why or why not?

7. From my point of view, is the world an angrier place than it used to be? If so, what has contributed to its becoming this way? If not, what has apparently led some people to believe differently than I do on the subject?

8. Do I have a problem with anger? If so, how serious is it? What has contributed to it? What can I do about it? What would help me the most in solving it? Does anyone I know and respect/love have a problem with anger? If so, is it an important issue in my relationship with him or her? Do I contribute to the problem in any way? What could I do to be of greatest help? What cautions, if any, should I take in expressing care and offering my help?

9. What kinds of anger do I have (*a*) the option, (*b*) the right, and/or (*c*) the responsibility to act upon and not act upon?

10. If I were to follow Jesus' teachings on anger more consistently in my life, what changes would I have to make?

From the self-examination that journal keeping with these kinds of questions opens up, we can learn more effective ways of managing our anger, come to a better understanding of other peoples' feelings and expressions of anger, and become less judgmental both of ourselves and of them in the process.

GETTING MORE ANGER OUT

The first vignette presented in this book narrated the frustrating experience of a woman named Rhea in a grocery store checkout line that closed just as her turn arrived. Rhea, we recall, chose not to express openly the displeasure she felt as she was forced to move her cart over to the next aisle. Though her behavior in this situation was consistent with her general approach to expressing anger, we wondered whether she might be doing herself at least some disservice by her practice of holding her irritations in, instead of letting more of them out.

Rhea and many like her have two primary reasons for keeping angry feelings private. One is to prevent further unpleasant feelings from arising, in oneself and/or in others. Rhea went on later to say to her neighbor Sue: *If I complained to the clerk or to the manager, they might get mad back, and then we'd all be feeling bad.* The other reason for refraining from expressing angry feelings is to avoid conflict. When pressed further by Sue to approach the store clerk, Rhea responded: *What would be the point? Nothing will come of it except a lot of defensiveness and arguing that won't get us anywhere.*

Rhea seems prepared to endure a great deal of displeasure and irritation in her life rather than let her angry feelings be known to anyone else. She has every right to make this choice, for herself, whatever anyone else may think about it, particularly if she also believes strongly that most conflicts do not get resolved satisfactorily. Rhea sees no problem with her chosen way of dealing with anger. Sometimes, she does say to her friends that they ought to "get along by going along more" and finds their disagreeing with her distasteful, but for the most part Rhea is clear that her decision is right for her, though it may not be for someone else.

Is there anything that a caring person either can or ought to do for someone who tries to handle anger the way Rhea does? One response is to feel comfortable about not doing anything. Until this relatively benign approach to anger becomes a problem for a particular person, any help offered to him or her is not likely to be accepted. There is, however, another response, one that respects the wisdom of the first one: affirm the normalcy of feeling irritated about genuine irritations and invite a response. One pastor suggested doing it this way: *That must have really gotten to you. I'd have really been fuming, at least for a minute or two, over that.* Neither response makes any demand on an angry person to act differently on the basis of the anger than he or she has already chosen to do. Both, however, convey a respect for the importance of acknowledging to ourselves the anger that we do feel.

Acknowledging the anger can be quite important, as the following case demonstrates. At a support group meeting with fellow lay ministers of pastoral care one evening, Jack let out some of his growing frustration working with Tom: *He's angry as all get-out—I know he is—but I'm having a lot of trouble getting him to admit it.* Tom's father died of a sudden heart attack just as the two were beginning to enjoy a new level of mutual respect and affection in their relationship.

Grief stricken, Tom nevertheless quickly and competently assumed the mantle of primary caretaker for his mother, with the gratitude and support of his three siblings. Jack has been very supportive of Tom since the funeral and hopes that some of his own experiences mourning the deaths of both his parents might prove comforting and helpful to his new care receiver.

Because he has "been there" himself, Jack recognizes all too well the signs of unexpressed anger that Tom is beginning to show. Tom fidgets more during their conversations and often interrupts Jack in midsentence. Tom reports being more short-tempered around his wife and children, and with mild embarrassment, he admits that several of his church friends have begun gently teasing him about how cranky he is these days. Jack is concerned: *I know what holding my anger in did to me, and I don't want the same thing to happen to Tom.* He is also thinking that in his last conversation with Tom, he made a mistake in the way he handled things. The interchange that Jack sketched went as follows:

> **Tom:** *My out-of-sorts-ness is not really all that big a deal, Jack. It's just that I've got a lot on my mind these days, making sure that Mom's going to be all right.*
>
> **Jack:** *I think you're kidding yourself, old buddy. You've got a whole bunch of mad down there about your dad's dying on you, and you're getting it out in all the wrong ways.*
>
> **Tom:** *What are you talking about?*

Jack's peers did not hesitate to affirm his self-assessment. Though sincerely motivated in his belief about what was in Tom's best interest long term, Jack still "jumped the gun," as one peer shepherd put it. He came on too strong, before Tom was even ready to acknowledge his anger, much less to deal with it. Jack agreed. *When we get together again,* he said, *I'm going to apologize for what I said and tell Tom that at the time I was probably speaking more about myself than about him.*

When Jack carried through on his plan, he received a somewhat surprising reaction from Tom: *Yeah, you really hacked me off for a minute there, Jack. But you know what? I've thought more about what you said this week, and though I don't like to admit it, I think you're probably right.* Jack's next response contributed greatly to getting the work with his care receiver back on track:

Jack: *You're being very generous with me, Tom, and I appreciate it. Tell me, though, what is there about that anger that you say is hard to admit?*

Tom: *Well, it's stupid. Dad didn't die to make me unhappy; he didn't have any choice about it at all. How can I be angry about something like that?*

Jack: *When I got so angry after my folks were gone, I knew that it wasn't their fault or anything like that, but knowing it still didn't make me feel any less angry. It still seemed like somehow they died because they were mad at me or something and did it to punish me.*

Tom: *Yeah, that went through my head, too. Are we both just crazy, then?*

Jack: *I don't really think so. Logically, it doesn't make a whole lot of sense to think the way we've been talking about, but emotionally is something else.*

Tom: *What do you mean?*

Jack: *Blaming someone for dying on us can be a way of telling ourselves that they're still here. After all, we're fussing at them, and we wouldn't be if they were gone!*

Tom: *You know, funny as that sounds, there's a relieflike quality to it. Just for a minute, it keeps me from feeling so down-and-out sad that Dad is gone.*

Jack: *I don't know about you, Tom, but for me, being mad is usually easier to deal with than being sad.*

Tom: *That fits me, too, now that I think about it. Maybe I've gotten so cranky just to keep from crying so much.*

Jack: *How do people react when you do cry about this?*

Tom: *A whole lot better than when I'm short-tempered with them!*

Jack: *I think I'd stick with crying.*

Tom: *Absolutely. But when I'm by myself, I'm gonna be more honest about having a few angry feelings from time to time.*

Jack: *Sounds like a plan to me.*

Many forms of anger are excessive in their outward manifestations. As such, they challenge us to learn and practice various techniques of *restraint*. Restraining the way we express our anger, however, ought never to be at the expense of honest acknowledgment of the anger in the first place. We cannot restrain our anger well unless we have already acknowledged that we are feeling it. We do, of course, have available to us a mechanism for driving the anger we feel out of awareness altogether: *repression*. However, in the long run, making use of it only makes things worse. As Tom's actions amply illustrate, when we deny our anger to ourselves, that anger begins to exert its influence on our behavior all on its own, unmediated by conscious deliberation and choice, and soon slips out of our control. For Tom, the result was the very opposite of what he intended. Rather than making a conscious decision to keep to himself something he believed unworthy of him, he allowed the unconscious part of his psyche to repress the unwanted anger. As a consequence, he lost any further power to make any decisions about it and became a mere conduit for the anger to release itself on its own terms.

Jack's first effort at leading his care receiver to acknowledge previously denied anger almost failed. Too abrupt, he adopted a position of superior knowledge about what was going on in Tom's heart. Instead of telling Tom that he had a lot of anger in him, Jack would have been more helpful had he invited Tom to make the discovery himself; for example: *All this short-temperedness and crankiness isn't like you, Tom. What do you think it might be about?* Jack's initial blunder, however, did not seriously impede progress in the shepherding relationship because (1) he quickly took responsibility for his mistake, and (2) he had already won Tom's trust. Blunder though it was, Jack's comments about Tom's anger nevertheless reflected some hard-won insights about feeling anger in the midst of grief. We grieve because we suffer loss. As is the case with any kind of deprivation, anger is a normal, expectable accompaniment. Telling ourselves that it is "stupid" to feel the anger we do feel will not make the anger go away. Encouraging someone we care about to accept his or her angry feelings instead of denying them is one important way of honoring the God-given capacity to experience and deal with anger that is in all of us.

KEEPING MORE ANGER IN

In a perfect world, getting angry would accomplish only constructive purposes. First, our anger would accurately signal a clearly identifiable feeling of deprivation. Then, it would enlist our faculties of discrimination and judgment to determine whether this feeling is provoked by real or imagined deprivation. Finally, our anger would provide much of the energy needed either for alleviating the real need or for reevaluating the imagined one. In a perfect world, since all anger would lead only to positive outcomes, it would always be a good thing to express any and every feeling of anger as it occurs.

Ours, however, is not a perfect world. In the actual world, getting angry serves constructive purposes and leads to positive outcomes only some of the time. At other times, anger signals more confusion than clarity about real and imaginary deprivations. It demands expression more for its own sake than for the sake of satisfying the need behind it and turns us toward blaming others for frustrations that we mostly bring upon ourselves. Finally, anger fuels chronic irritability at the expense of relationships that otherwise could foster compassionate understanding, forgiveness, and genuine give-and-take.

What do these observations imply for expressing our anger? The single most important implication is this: we are justified in giving expression to our anger when we are prepared to let our anger do its proper work of signaling feelings of deprivation, determining whether the deprivation is real or imagined, and alleviating the real need or reevaluating the imagined one. This is not to say that every feeling of anger that, as we have seen, always wells up within as an involuntary reaction to some feeling of deprivation can be brought under the sway of reason and careful judgment about its expression. It is to say, however, that we have within us the power to choose how we will and will not express the anger that we feel, and that we bear the God-given responsibility to exercise that power of choice wisely.

Wise choices about expressing anger are those that proceed from a prior determination that our anger signals a real and important need. They incorporate evidence that our need is occasioned by others' offensive or harmful actions and not self-destructive behaviors of our own. Finally, these choices restrict our expression of anger only to those who have contributed to our need and/or to those who can help us satisfy it. Many of our choices about expressing anger are anything but wise in these senses. Instead, they reduce us to venting displeasure at imagined or unimportant insults and injuries, to blaming others for what we have brought on ourselves, and to spewing venom on people who have done nothing to contribute to our problems and who are not in a position to alleviate them.

Sue, whom we encountered in the first chapter with Rhea and Belle, is a firm advocate of letting people know in no uncertain terms whenever they do something that irritates or offends her. Mild concern about her reputation for outspokenness apparently does not deter Sue very much from giving people a good piece of her mind when she sees fit.

Interestingly, though, Sue also shows clear ability to pull her punches with people to whom, for whatever reason, Sue decides it best to be cordial. Like Rhea, however, Sue shows little willingness to reconsider anything about her way of dealing with anger, particularly along the lines (1) of distinguishing important from unimportant offenses, and (2) of assessing the impact of her expectations of others on the degree of frustration she feels with them. Therefore, any guiding that someone might offer Sue should focus, for the time being at least, on other issues. Nevertheless, there are ways to open up the possibility of discussing other approaches to expressing anger, as the following (imaginary) exchange illustrates:

Caregiver: *So you do watch what you say a little bit, around a few people at least. Why is that?*

Sue: *Well, we can't afford to get our bosses mad at us, can we? [laughing] And I wouldn't want my priest giving me trouble some day at the pearly gates! And if I ever get my daughter-in-law going, there'd be no end to it. She's even feistier than I am.*

Caregiver: *I remember your saying how impatient you get with your friend Rhea over all the irritations that she holds inside herself. But maybe you're just a little more like her than you think.*

Sue: *How in the world could that be?*

Caregiver: *Well, you're saying that sometimes you can avoid conflict by keeping angry feelings to yourself. I wonder if that maybe isn't Rhea's philosophy, too.*

Sue: *I really hadn't thought of it that way. I guess the real difference between Rhea and me is that she wants to avoid conflict more than I do.*

Caregiver: *That may be so. That would make it more a matter of degree.*

Sue: *Maybe Rhea and I should try to figure out how to split the differences in our approaches.*

Caregiver: *Now there's an idea!*

Though some of Sue's friends regard her approach to expressing frustration as shoot-from-the-hip, Sue herself seems quite competent to decide before she acts, to weigh the purposes served both by letting her anger show and by keeping it to herself, and to reserve its expression for situations in which something important is at stake. Positive reinforcement of these competencies is the best way of encouraging their further development and application.

With respect to the specific situation cited earlier, Sue does have a reason to be irritated with her friend. In a grocery store checkout line, her neighbor has suffered the same kind of frustration that all of us suffer from time to time. Rhea has not been treated well by a fatigued and possibly overworked clerk. Sue is correct in her judgment that since the offending clerk is the major source of the frustration, he is the one to whom Rhea's frustration should be expressed. Though Rhea did not complain to Sue about the incident, were she to do so without first attempting to deal with it at its source, she would be taking out her anger inappropriately on someone who cannot do anything to rectify the situation.

On target as some of Sue's convictions are, her overall assessment of the situation seems flawed in two ways. First, she does not acknowledge that everyday frustrations are sometimes made worse by our own attitudes and actions. Having to wait longer to pay for our groceries is more irksome, as Rhea discovered, when we have added shopping to an already too heavy morning or afternoon schedule. Also, such inconveniences can become minor crises when we bring to them the thoroughly indefensible conviction that our own contentment is more important than anyone else's and should, therefore, be assured first.

The second way in which Sue's assessment is flawed stems from her overevaluation of the particular incident's importance. In other words, she is making too big a deal out of a very small transgression. Though the checker's treatment of Rhea certainly was less than it ought to have been, expressing as much irritation as Sue does about it is out of proportion to the nature of the offense. In situations like this, Sue needs to learn how to keep more of her anger in and to reserve letting more of it out for situations that really do call for its expression in no uncertain terms. Sue is more than capable of doing both. And so are we.

CONCLUSION AND TRANSITION

Much of the anger that most people feel, in a great variety of circumstances, is like the anger that Rhea and Sue felt in the very mundane setting of a neighborhood grocery store. This anger of displeasure, irritation, and frustration usually flares up and burns down quickly, with little or no residue left behind. Some people choose as their rule of thumb for dealing with such anger a combination of "not sweating the little things," "letting bygones be bygones," "putting it out of mind," "forgetting about it," and, in other familiar words, "not making mountains out of molehills." Others insist that the right way to deal even with mild irritations is to register them clearly with whoever may be provoking them to ensure that the offense will not be repeated and that, as a consequence, they will not be burdened with as much anger as they might be otherwise.

Though we may disagree among ourselves about which of these approaches to expressing "normal" anger is the better one, there really is no good reason for anyone to insist that his or her own preference in the matter should be the norm for everyone else. For the most part, the two approaches reflect fundamentally different attitudes toward maintaining relationships, which, in themselves, have merit and which, in any event, are difficult to change. It can put strain on a particular relationship if one partner subscribes to the first approach and the other to the second, especially if that partner demands that the other look at things the way he or she does. Nevertheless, differing attitudes and ways of dealing with conflict are hardly lethal to any relationship, given mutual respect and a willingness to compromise. In general, in the rounds of everyday life, the normal kinds of anger all of us feel get dealt with reasonably effectively, and we move on. Not all anger submits to such relatively easy management, however, as the next chapters will make plain.

6 Getting beyond Grudges and Paybacks

FOR ALL THEIR APPARENT DIFFERENCES, ANGRY FEELINGS AND expressions differ more in degree than in kind, even as they reflect a common originating process. Thus, looking at anger in terms of an imagined continuum on which we place what we deem normal and not-so-normal feelings and expressions of anger ensures that we take adequately into account (1) the relative degrees of intensity of the feelings under consideration, (2) the appropriateness of the feelings to the circumstances occasioning them, (3) the varying extents to which the feelings are hidden from or made overt to others, and (4) the level of responsibility exhibited in translating those feelings into actions. With the idea of a continuum as background, this chapter focuses on dealing with two kinds of anger that lie just beyond the "normal" range of angry feelings.

The first section of the chapter focuses on the ruminating kind of anger that is fed by stored memories of past wrongs. Then the chapter turns to anger that does not remain harbored merely inwardly, but constantly tallies others' offenses as the basis for seeking revenge of some sort. In this section, the envisioned acts of "getting even" are relatively benign in character. We leave for treatment in a subsequent chapter the difficulties of showing care for people whose penchant for vengeance takes on an intensity and destructiveness beyond their ability to control.

LETTING GO OF KEEPING SCORE

In our earlier narration of the unpleasant event in a grocery store, we introduced Belle, whom we characterized as a chronic complainer. That is, in words reminiscent of the apostle Paul, she persistently keeps score of wrongs (cf. 1 Corinthians 13:5, REB). Her resulting resentfulness and bitterness have made it inevitable that, for all her intentions to the contrary, Belle will continue to put off even some of her closest friends. Ironically, others' distancing merely provides Belle with one more thing to complain about, instead of serving as the impetus for her to make changes in herself.

Shortly after her conversation with Sue, which was reported earlier, Belle suffered the loss of her husband, sister, and grandson—all within a matter of months. Wisely, she asked her pastor for a lay shepherd from the congregation to help her with her grief. Also wisely, the pastor selected someone whom he believed could deal with chronic anger as well as with grief. Although the lay shepherd, whom I will call Zoe, gave Belle significant help in dealing with both issues, the following discussion will lift up some of the things that she did in response to Belle's many expressions of grudge-anger.

Unlike many of Belle's acquaintances, Zoe allowed herself to listen patiently to one tirade after another from her care receiver in the interest, first, of gaining a better understanding of the roots of the anger expressed and, second, of forming and revising as necessary her strategy for responding to the quite predictable next round of fulminations. The following dialogue, beginning with an outburst from Belle, gives us a glimpse of how Zoe began her work:

> **Belle:** *You're darned right I'm mad! That doctor should have kept after Bill [her husband] for smoking and drinking after his first heart attack. And they should have gotten rid of that cranky horse before Annie [her sister] could get thrown by it. And my son should never have let Jerry [her grandson] drive the tractor on that muddy road. They all knew better.*
> **Zoe:** *You're hurting, and it's their fault.*

Belle: *That's a pretty hateful thing to say.*

Zoe: *Are you hearing judgment in my voice?*

Belle: *No, not really. But you don't sound like you think much of what I've been saying.*

Zoe: *Belle, you're mad at them for things you think they've done to your loved ones as well as to you, and you think they somehow did them deliberately.*

Belle: *And you don't like me to talk like that.*

Zoe: *Do you think it makes sense to talk like that?*

Belle: *[pauses thoughtfully] Okay, they didn't do what they did on purpose. But are you saying I shouldn't be mad at all?*

Zoe: *No, I'm saying that being mad this way isn't going to get you anywhere but just staying mad.*

Belle: *All my friends tell me I am mad all the time.*

Zoe: *Are they right?*

At this point in their work together, Zoe is directing a respectful but forceful invitation to Belle to examine the pattern of her chronic anger to help her find alternative ways of holding, expressing, and working through her feelings. As this brief interchange shows, one of the things that keeps Belle "mad all the time" is her constant looking for someone to blame for her deprivations and her blaming people who are not really part of the problem:

Zoe: *It looks to me like you've got to find somebody to blame for these tragic deaths. If you're going to do that, though, do you really think you've found the right people?*

Belle: *What do you mean?*

Zoe: *From what you've told me, it sounds like your husband, sister, and grandson all did some things that they shouldn't have done.*

Belle: *I should blame them instead?*

Zoe: *Well, if you've got to blame somebody, I guess you could start there.*

Belle: *What would that accomplish?*

Zoe: *Good question. I wonder myself if blame really helps all that much, no matter who may deserve it.*

Belle: *A lot of the times when I'm angry I know I'm looking for anybody to blame, no matter who it is.*
Zoe: *Well, that sure is one way to stay angry, isn't it?*
Belle: *And drive people away to boot. I really don't like having so few friends, you know.*

By suggesting that blaming is a way of staying angry, Zoe hopes to prod Belle to acknowledge that both her faultfinding and her anger might be serving a larger purpose than merely maintaining a scorecard of others' insults and injuries. What Zoe is looking for is a readiness on her care receiver's part to get more into her underlying feelings of pain and loss, instead of covering them over with angry outbursts against one scapegoat after another. It would have been especially gratifying to Zoe had Belle responded by saying something like, *Why do I want to stay angry like this all the time, Zoe?*

As care receivers often do, however, Belle chooses not to walk the path to which her lay shepherd was pointing. Instead of opening herself to some of the deeper feelings of deprivation that lie below the surface of her anger, she steers the conversation to the less threatening subject of why other people do not like her. Pleased, however, that her care receiver now seems willing to take some responsibility for the quality of her relationships, Zoe quickly shifts gears to follow Belle down this new path:

Zoe: *Thanks for your honesty. It really does hurt not to have more friends. Do people who know you realize that you're hurting about this?*
Belle: *Probably not. Most of them see me as somebody who couldn't care less whether they want a relationship with me or not.*
Zoe: *Looks like you've done a pretty good number on them.*
Belle: *And an even bigger one on myself.*
Zoe: *Are you saying that you're part of the problem here, and not just them?*
Belle: *I'm a big part of the problem. If I'd quit complaining so much, I know I'd have more friends. But right now I don't know how to keep myself from going on and on about things that don't really matter. I've been doing it for too long, I guess.*

Delighted with the progress of the conversation, Zoe next encourages Belle to do something about her frustration rather than to continue dwelling on it. However, she does not do this without determining in advance whether Belle is indeed ready to move on: *Want a suggestion?* she asks. Hoping for a positive response, Zoe nevertheless is prepared to accept a negative one from her care receiver, without wavering in her commitment to accept whatever state of mind Belle might be in. This time Belle chooses to accept Zoe's offer:

Belle: *Please, anything!*

Zoe: *Instead of complaining about what people do, why not find things to compliment them on?*

Belle: *That would be a switch, wouldn't it?*

Zoe: *I think you'll like the results. For me, anyway, it's easier to stop doing something if I start doing something else instead.*

When Belle began to put Zoe's suggestion into practice, she was surprised by her friends' reactions. Though initially puzzled and on their guard, they very soon began responding very positively to their friend's new initiative. One said to Belle: *At first, I didn't know what to do with all this "make nice" coming from you. But you know what? I like it! And I like you a lot better since you started doing it. Don't stop!* As things continued to improve between Belle and her friends, she found more energy to work on changing her predilection to treat relatively trivial deprivations, such as unintended slights by distracted store clerks, on a par with serious ones, such as the searing losses she now confronts. Now, she is pleased with the way she is substituting the application of the "think and say something nice" principle for more and more of her blaming behaviors.

Aware that her shepherding relationship with Belle is coming to an end, Zoe continues to pray that her care receiver will eventually acknowledge that harboring grudges is her way of protecting herself from facing underlying hurt, especially the pain of significant loss. Otherwise, Zoe believes, Belle could fall back into her old way of thinking about her life as filled with more than a fair share of frustrations for which she deserves compensation instead of pressure to change her own attitudes and behavior. From such a standpoint, it will be increasingly difficult for Belle to work through a lot of her grief. Nevertheless, Zoe and her peer lay shepherds agreed, Belle had come a long way, and for that, they can be thankful.

Zoe's admirable work with a grieving but also chronically angry care receiver witnesses powerfully to the possibility of changing long-standing, maladaptive patterns of dealing with anger. Sadly, however, many care receivers are not as open to change as Belle. As a consequence, their caregivers may see less growth in them than Zoe anticipates seeing in Belle. These hard truths should remind us that, as caring Christians, our primary task is only to invite change; for example: *You've been carrying around a lot of anger about a lot of things for a long time. Want to lighten the load?* Our care receivers or our family members or our friends must choose for themselves whether to accept the invitation or not. If their response is positive, and if they do make positive changes in themselves, we must also remind ourselves constantly that it will be due less to the guiding that we do and far more to what God does through us.

LETTING GO OF GETTING EVEN

Though we may not recognize it at first glance, the kind of grudge harboring that we just saw in Belle is a good bit similar to the drive to retaliate that we earlier encountered in the young man we called Steve. A coworker with Frank on a sensitive project, Steve is angry about a colleague's violation of a confidence. Steve threatened not only to stay mad at Jerry but also to get even with him. In one important respect, of course, Belle's anger is quite different from Steve's. She is content merely to complain, while Steve cannot rest until he carries out a payback of some kind. Nevertheless, Belle's and Steve's anger do share something important in common: fantasies about evening an imaginary "score." Where they differ is in the expression of their respective fantasy-filled anger. As Belle dwells inwardly on her fantasies, Steve acts outwardly on his.

With this latter consideration, we are in a position to make another comparison. Steve's way of dealing with anger bears some resemblance not only to Belle's; it also bears more than just a little resemblance to that of the driver, whom we will now call Nat, who became enraged at a young woman in front of him and almost ran her off the road. Nat believes, as does Steve, that there is someone out there who has something coming to him or her and that he alone has the right to administer the needed "justice." The justice that Nat, unlike Steve, has in mind is purely aggressive and wholly destructive, reminiscent of Lamech's boast in the Book of Genesis:

> "Adah and Zillah, listen to me;
> wives of Lamech, mark what I say:
> I kill a man for wounding me,
> a young man for a blow.
> If sevenfold vengeance was to be exacted for Cain,
> for Lamech it would be seventy-sevenfold."
> —Genesis 4:23-24, REB

Though it is not clear just what sort of retaliation Steve has in mind for Jerry, more than likely it will take the form of getting Jerry in the same kind of trouble that Jerry's thoughtlessness created for Frank and himself. In this respect, Steve's operating principle comes closer to the "eye for an eye, tooth for a tooth" position that we discussed earlier. As harsh as this principle may seem to Christians saved by grace, it is nevertheless a more responsible approach to expressing anger than Nat's is ever likely to be. At the heart of Nat's anger is evil—righteous outrage mutated to the dark side. As different as Nat's and Steve's actions are, however, there is also a common spirit about them: vengeance.

In chapter 4, we discovered that underlying every form of anger is some kind of perceived deprivation, real or imagined. What kind of deprivations create a disposition to seek revenge at every perceived slight, offense, or wrong? The principal source of the disposition is deprivation, beginning early in life, that we feel powerless to overcome. Usually, the experiences of such deprivation are so painful that we go to great lengths not to be reminded of them at all. But reminded we must be, as the normal slights, offenses, and wrongs that afflict everyone at some time or other in life eventually take their toll on us, too. Seeking revenge for a present insult is a way to stave off remembering other insults that we suffered once upon a time and could do nothing about. These considerations can help us to understand both the persistence of revenge seeking in both Nat and Steve and the very considerable differences in the way each pursues it.

The intense, out-of-control nature of Nat's vengeful behaviors strongly suggests that he has had to struggle with many painful and humiliating experiences for a very long time. His powerlessness in the face of those experiences has made him overly sensitive to even the slightest hint that anyone, at any time, might be trying to get the better of him. In popular parlance, Nat has a "short fuse" or is a "walking time bomb." Anything that in any way reminds him of past insults and injuries can set him off. Steve, by contrast, does not allow his anger to get the better of him so much that he becomes unable to plan carefully his responses to perceived offenses. He is as vulnerable to feeling taken advantage of as Nat is, but, unlike Nat, he is not crippled by too many reminders of too many past outrages. Steve has likely suffered enough unjust deprivations growing up to find revenge for present insults a pleasing prospect, but because he is not as wounded as Nat is, his retaliations are not as extreme as Nat's.

It might be tempting to conclude that we must somehow cut Nat and Steve some "slack" because of the injustices under which each has been forced to live. We must resist any such temptation. The fact that strong feelings do, in Steve's case sometimes and in Nat's case most times, get in the way of their expressing anger constructively does not for a moment absolve the two men from responsibility for appropriate behavior. Like the rest of us, they too must eventually accept the fact that burying angry feelings from the past by seeking revenge for present slights is a very ineffective way of dealing with anger. No sooner do we drive out of awareness one set of unpleasant memories than some new insult arouses other ones, and the desperation to get even pours over us all over again. Unchecked, retaliatory behaviors can escalate all too easily from the relatively benign form that we see in Steve to the frighteningly destructive form embodied in Nat that ruins lives.

Whether we are speaking about the Steves of the world or the Nats, a better way of dealing with deprivation-induced anger and rage exists than the way of retaliation and destruction. From the law codes of the Old Testament through the teachings of Jesus to the apostle Paul and the writer of the Letter to the Hebrews, the Scriptures consistently present a single, nonnegotiable truth for all of us. Stated with stark simplicity, the truth is that vengeance belongs to God alone:

Thou shalt not avenge, nor bear any grudge against the children of thy people, but thou shalt love thy neighbour as thyself: I am the LORD. *(Leviticus 19:18,* KJV*)*

"You have heard that they were told, 'Love your neighbour and hate your enemy.' But what I tell you is this: Love your enemies and pray for your persecutors." (Matthew 5:43-44, REB*)*

Never try to get revenge; leave that, my friends, to God's anger. As Scripture says: Vengeance is mine—I will pay them back, the Lord promises. But there is more: If your enemy is hungry, you should give him food, and if he is thirsty, let him drink. Thus you heap red-hot coals on his head. (Romans 12:19-20, JB*)*

For we know who said, "I will take revenge, I will repay"; and who also said, "The Lord will judge his people." (Hebrews 10:30, GNB*)*

In light of these texts, the better way of dealing with the temptation to get even with someone can be stated in just one word: *forgiveness.* According to the Scriptures, forgiveness is a deliberate choosing not to hold another's offensive or hurtful actions toward us against him or her. We make this choice for the sake of a reconciled relationship, if not now, at least at sometime in the future. Instead of our paying someone back, as we may believe justice properly demands, God is calling us to make ourselves vulnerable to even greater hurt by first letting go of the very claim on another that the other's hurtful action(s) may warrant. One lay shepherd, Ann, guided her care receiver, Polly, toward a more forgiving stance in the following way:

Polly: *I know I'm not supposed to act this way, being a Christian and all, but Lynette just keeps on criticizing me to our boss behind my back, and I've had all I can take. She's not perfect either, and I'm going to make sure that Alex [the boss] finds out. Two can play this game, you know.*

Ann: *Yes, two can play the game, but is it really the game you want to play?*

Polly: *Right now, it sure is!*

Ann: *I'm sure that's the way it seems to you right now, Polly.*

It isn't like you, though, to get into backbiting stuff like that, even when someone's taking a nip or two out of you.

Polly: *I guess you're going to lay on me the "forgive your enemies" thing now. And I guess I know I should, but I want to get even so bad that I really don't know how to begin to do the forgiveness bit.*

Ann: *Well, one way might be to start recalling times when you did things you needed to be forgiven for and were forgiven.*

Polly: *I can do that. But Lynette sure isn't going to, and she'll never even think about apologizing to me, much less asking for my forgiveness.*

Ann: *When you received forgiveness, did you always have to ask for it?*

Polly: *Now that you mention it, no. But do you mean I've just got to go up to that woman and blurt out that I forgive her?*

Ann: *Is that the way it worked in your own case?*

Polly: *Well, no. They didn't say anything to me; they just treated me better, and somehow I knew I was all right with them.*

Ann: *What do you suppose might happen if you did something like that to Lynette?*

Polly: *Probably nothing much would change in her. But maybe I would feel better.*

Ann: *Sounds like a pretty good deal to me.*

Not counting the trespasses of others against them is our first step toward moving beyond a spirit of bitterness and retaliation. The second step is replacing resentment with love. In this context, it is important to keep in mind that love is not a particular sort of feeling; we are not called to love those who seek our harm in the sense of developing emotional "warm fuzzies" toward them. What God asks of us, instead, is that we actively seek those others' genuine good, making personal sacrifices if necessary, no matter how strongly they may demean, defame, or harm us and no matter how negative we may feel toward them for doing so. The fundamental reason for our being called to do so is that this is the way that God has chosen to deal with us. As God forgives our own sins and offenses against heaven, God calls us to forgive others' sins and offenses against us. As God seeks our perfection in the image of Christ, in spite of our resistance to divine grace, God calls us to serve God's own purposes for others, whether they are ready to respond to God's love or not.

SUMMARY

We bring this chapter to a close with an especially powerful illustration of what forgiveness can mean, this time in an extreme situation.

As Danny was being led from his cell on death row to the room where he would be put to death by lethal injection, the mother of the young woman he raped and murdered years ago stood outside the prison in the company of other protestors against capital punishment. With them, Katie sang quietly in the darkness, holding her flickering candle, while tears streamed down her face. At the same time, her husband, Charlie, sat with other observers next door to the execution room.

Katie and Charlie are keenly aware of how much they have grown together, both physically and spiritually, to be at the places they now occupy. During Danny's trial, all they could think of was their daughter's untimely, outrageous, painful death and of the retribution her memory so fully deserved. Now, they are grateful for the patient listening, supporting, and guiding of the lay shepherd who has been with them from the beginning and who now is one of their dearest friends. Katie and Charlie have come to the state prison on this dreadful day with two purposes in mind. One is to witness in the name of their faith that taking a life, including that of the man who murdered their own daughter, is no solution to anything. And the other is to ensure that the last words Danny will know in this life will be from them. Charlie could only mouth them through the window that separated him from the dying prisoner: "We forgive you. Go with God."

We cannot know whether Danny fully understood the message. Before losing consciousness altogether, he looked into Charlie's eyes and smiled tenderly. As Charlie later told it, in that brief moment he and Danny were one, in their tears.

7 Toward the Extremes: Fury, Rage, and Hate

THERE HAVE ALWAYS BEEN SOME VERY ANGRY CHRISTIAN PEOPLE IN the world. The God-intended anger that they feel arises from the recognition of truly horrendous deprivations that threaten the well-being, dignity, and future possibilities of human beings as children of God. Any adequate list of such deprivations would include, at the very least, poverty, world hunger, war, racism, sexism, neglect, abuse, assaults on the environment, and preventable diseases. Regarding such deprivations as these, it is appropriate not only that we feel anger from time to time but also that we become very angry people who will not rest until the deprivations are overcome, for ourselves and for our brothers and sisters everywhere.

Tragically for the mission of the people of God, though, most of the anger in our pews today, including our own anger, is not of this sort. Rather, it is anger that has no good reason for being. Instead of manifesting the zeal of true servants of God, it reflects (1) mundane self-centeredness, (2) intolerance of the normal frustrations that accompany everyday life, and (3) unwillingness to balance personal whims, goals, and plans with the responsibilities attending mutually satisfying relationships. In this somber assessment, however, there is also good news to be found. A great deal of our anger is anger that we are quite capable of managing and even overcoming. What is needed, first, is a commitment to understand ourselves as angry people more adequately. Then, in order to make changes for the better in the ways we express our anger, we must seek the help of patient listeners who are unafraid to challenge us.

Having acknowledged this much, we still must face the fact that not all the news about anger in our society and churches is good news. Some of it is distressing and discouraging, and it forces us to confront very painful truths. The first is that in moments of extreme frustration, anger can get the better of people and drive them to say and do things that they can neither take back nor make right. Another is that, given enough deprivation over enough time, people can become enslaved by a vicious kind of anger that aims only at destroying others. Finally, vulnerability to both temporary fits of temper and to long-standing, vehement, hurtful anger is as evident in the pews of our churches as it is on the streets and back alleys of our neighborhoods. Fury, rage, and hate are everywhere. The purpose of the chapter is to explore their pervasiveness and its implications for how we can minister even to very angry people in the name of Christ.

TAMING THE FURIES

We have already looked fury fully in the face, watching Bill, the frustrated father of Mark, explode with outrage during his son's softball game. Unlike people who seem capable of one furious outburst after another without a hint of self-recrimination, Bill showed nothing less than outright mortification following his own tirade: *I'm so ashamed of myself that I don't think I can ever show my face to these parents again. And most of them are my friends! What am I gonna do? What's wrong with me?* That Bill could say this much so candidly about his behavior is, we noted, a very positive sign. Bill feels badly enough about what he did not to want it to happen again. He not only acknowledged his hair-trigger temper in words; he also took positive action to overcome it. He reached out to his friends, admitted that he needed to change, and asked for their support.

To pick up the story again: in the process of taming his fury, Bill sought out for advice as well as for support one friend in particular, whom I will call Howard. Bill picked Howard because he is a respect-ed lay shepherd in Bill's church and because Bill knows that Howard is the kind of friend who will not let him off the hook easily. As the following exchange demonstrates, Bill made a very wise choice:

Howard: *I can tell you're shaken up over what you did back there. But aren't you leaving out somebody who's pretty important to the whole picture?*

Bill: *What do you mean?*

Howard: *I'm thinking about Mark. It must have awfully hard on him, too, seeing his dad make a fool of himself in front of all of his friends.*

Bill: *I apologized to Mark. He's okay with it.*

Howard: *Maybe he is, Bill, but what I'm wondering about is why you are so okay with it.*

Bill: *I'm not okay with it. I feel terrible about what I did.*

Howard: *Terrible to your friends. But terrible to Mark? I don't get a sense of the kind of embarrassment you're talking about when you describe what's going on between you and Mark.*

Bill: *You really aren't going to let me off any hooks, are you?*

Howard: *I don't think you want me to.*

Intense embarrassment is a very uncomfortable feeling. We want to get rid of it as quickly as possible. Because our friends' embarrass-ing moments can so easily stir up painful reminders of similar per-sonal experiences, we usually recoil from their pain just as fervently as we do from our own. In the interest of expediting their speedy recovery, and with it our own, we often proffer help that (1) discounts the seriousness of the situation provoking the embarrassment in the first place, (2) minimizes the feeling itself, and (3) gets in the way of anyone's learning anything important by means of our shared, God-given capacity to feel shame. By way of examples:

Oh, don't let it bother you. Those kids' league umpires never know what they're doing, anyway.

Hey, it's only a ball game. We're supposed to get crazy and upset, for heaven's sake.

No big deal! We all lose our temper sometimes.

All you need is a shower, a couple of beers, a good meal,

and you'll feel a whole lot better. By tomorrow, you won't remember what happened at all.

We all felt the same way over that call. That umpire has got to go.

Bill's lay shepherd says none of these things. Indeed, rather than offering Bill something right away to make him feel a little better, Howard deliberately brings up something that he knows will make Bill feel even worse. Why? Because he knows that, despite all the protestations to the contrary, Bill also wants to avoid as many of the consequences as he can of his truly shameful behavior. Further, Howard knows that it is precisely Bill's capacity to feel shame that will provide the motivation and energy that Bill needs to control his hot temper. By putting Mark in the picture, Howard reminds Bill that he has even more to be ashamed of than he has thus far admitted. Feeling appropriate shame, in all its fullness, offers Bill the best chance to make the changes he knows he must make. Like most of us, Bill will do almost anything to avoid feeling humiliated.

For many people today, appealing to a sense of shame to motivate behavioral change represents a throwback to a bygone era, which thought nothing of shaming people mercilessly, breaking spirits, and destroying hope. People carry around too many feelings of shame already, the argument goes, and as a result they believe that at the core of their being is something very bad. What they need is, not more reminders of what is wrong with them, but affirmations of their worth, dignity, goodness, capabilities, and possibilities. Thus, we should never say anything to anyone that would evoke a sense of embarrassment or shame, as in the following:

I am so disappointed in you.

You should be ashamed of yourself.

We don't do things like that in this family.

Instead, and again according to this point of view, we motivate behavioral change best by positive affirmations and reinforcements only; for example:

I'm so proud of you.

I know you didn't mean to do what you did deliberately.

That's the way to do it! Good job!

A good deal of truth rests in this way of looking at things. Countless numbers of human beings do suffer humiliation and self-loathing at the hands not only of the blatantly sadistic but also from the well-meaning who ooze conviction that breaking another's spirit is for that other person's greater good. Shaming that ends only with another's feeling worthless has no justification whatever, for it flies in the face of the most fundamental of all truths about us: We are created in the image of God and, as such, are of sacred and infinite worth. Affirming rather than shaming does, indeed, represent the better way to encourage people to make needed changes in themselves.

"Better," however, cannot mean "only." The basic flaw with exclusive affirmation is its partial, not complete, view of humankind. At the vital center of our being is a worthiness that is God's delight. Close to that vital center, however, exists also something else: a grandiose self-centeredness that refuses to acknowledge the sovereignty and goodness of the Creator, insisting on its own prerogatives above those of anyone else. In the traditional language of faith, we are at once images of God's glory and craven sinners. Or, in the word that Bill used about himself, there is something "wrong," indeed very wrong, about us. In many of the things we do, we are disappointments to our Creator, and we should be disappointments to ourselves. Our God-given capacity to feel shame, of the sort that Adam felt when he heard God's question "Adam, where are you?" is intended to force upon our awareness this seamier side of our nature so that we can begin doing whatever we need to do, with God's help, to change it for the better. To the shameless, however, such talk can only fall on deaf ears. We can be thankful that Bill's ears were not closed to the truth. What, however, if Bill refused to let himself be embarrassed about this genuinely embarrassing incident? Could Howard still be helpful to him? How might Howard proceed?

Most likely, in that eventuality, Howard would focus more on Bill's fears rather than on his shame. If Bill cannot feel the mortification that, as a responsible adult, he ought to feel about the uproar he created, he still may be reached through fears of what might happen in his life if he continues to allow his temper to run amok. Howard might begin by making an observation and follow it by asking Bill a question: *Well, Bill, I guess you aren't as concerned about this incident as I seem to be. Have you thought about what might happen if you keep on "losing it" whenever you feel like it?*

Under the assumption that Bill is, in the first place, invulnerable to feelings of shame, it is also possible that he is either indifferent to or oblivious of the effects of his behavior on others. In this eventuality, helping Bill bring to the surface whatever fears he may harbor about jeopardizing his future relationships will require an even stronger effort on Howard's part than keeping the focus just on Bill's embarrassment. More forcefully, Howard might say something like this: *I'm really worried about you, friend. If you keep going on like this, you can become a laughingstock to your friends, and even worse, you could lose your son's respect altogether.* We can easily imagine Bill's possible responses:

1. *I think you're blowing smoke, Howard. This isn't worth anybody's worrying about, much less my friends. And Mark's already forgotten about it.*

2. *That would really be bad, Howard; you and I know it would. I just can't imagine either thing happening, but I trust you, and if you're worried, then I guess I ought to be, too.*

The kind of response expressed in the second statement presumes a high level of trust already established in the shepherding relationship. In all likelihood, the only way that Howard can get through would be by means of the kind of challenging statement just quoted. But whether he does get through will depend heavily on whether Bill trusts him enough to take his words on faith until he can understand their wisdom for himself. As we will now see, some people do not seem capable of this level of trust at all. Because they are not, they put all of us at risk.

PROTECTING OURSELVES AND OTHERS AGAINST THE ENRAGED

Our world would be a much safer place if people could lose their tempers from time to time without doing any real damage in the process. A bitter taste in our mouths from swallowing another's insults might be an acceptable price to pay for maintaining a relationship with that person, if we could be assured that the insults would go no further. Unhappily, fury often does go further, much further, and we are all the worse for it. Though names can never really hurt, as the nursery rhyme reminds us, sticks and stones can. Pickup trucks and guns and very angry people can and do inflict serious and even permanent harm, no matter how hard we work at protecting ourselves and those we care about from them.

Recall the story of Patsy from chapter 2. Run off the road by an enraged driver, she came close to suffering injury and even death at the hands of someone whose uncontained fury quickly assumed a form far more malignant than that of merely blowing off steam in front of amused spectators. Instead, Patsy's nemesis expressed his fury violently and with destructive intent, putting her at a risk much greater than the risk to the umpire of Mark's softball game. Patsy's experience is one that more and more of us fear will happen to us. "Road rage" has become an especially potent symbol of the intense anger hovering over us these days, just waiting to be ignited.

Ours, we say repeatedly, is now an angry and violent society. Are more anger and violence surrounding us than in previous times? We in the relatively secure and comfortable Western world may lament that our communities seem more threatened than before, but across most of the planet other people have lived their lives for millennia facing daily dangers not all that much different from what they face today. Further, even a casual look at the history of our own heritage makes plain that things were rarely, if ever, better "once upon a time," the mythologies of Camelot and every other so-called golden age notwithstanding. Comparisons with former times, therefore, are hardly illuminating. What is important is our awareness that violent anger around us now cuts short many a life. This kind of anger demands our attention. To the faces of rage, how shall we, as Christians, respond?

We must, in whatever ways possible, protect ourselves, for we can be of no help to anyone by falling victim to another's out-of-control rage. Patsy understood this instinctively. She waited at the side of the road until the perpetrator was long out of view, counted her blessings, and then slowly proceeded back into town to report the incident, with as much of a description of the offending pickup truck as she could remember, hoping that her action might prevent the driver from doing harm to anyone else. It was frustrating for her to hear that the police could do little until an accident actually happens. Nevertheless, by putting the incident "in the hands of the law," Patsy said she was better able to put it out of her own mind. In another incident involving the same pickup truck driver, things did not go so well. The side-swiped driver, whose own truck was, in words he frequently used to his friends, "armed to the teeth," immediately took off in pursuit of his offender and received for his efforts a gunshot to the head, which killed him instantly. When rage begets more rage as the response, innocent parties are at even greater risk.

Most of us get through life without having to confront directly destructive rage very often, if at all. Further, it is highly unlikely that a lay shepherd will ever find himself or herself working with a truly enraged care receiver. In the first place, people with readily apparent rage should not be assigned to lay shepherds at all; they need professional interventions beyond the scope of lay caregiving. Second, lay shepherds whose care receivers are struggling with more manageable kinds of anger are in a position to see rage building up well before it overflows and, therefore, to begin the process, with the help of their peers and pastors, of early referral to a mental health professional. Of course, if a care receiver threatens to commit violent acts, all caregivers, lay and professional, have a duty to issue warnings to those at risk. Assuming such responsibility usually requires contacting law enforcement officers. In that event, should a lay shepherd continue to be the care receiver's primary helper? No. The lay shepherd should maintain the shepherding relationship at all only if his or her safety can be ensured. Enraged people are dangerous, and their potential to inflict harm upon us and upon others deserves our unwavering vigilance.

Does concern for our own well-being mean that lay shepherds, offering care in the name of Jesus Christ, have nothing to give to enraged people? Does it mean that we must remain so preoccupied with our own well-being that we never put ourselves in a position to express Christian concern to enraged people about theirs? Surely not. Even as Saul was "still breathing murderous threats against the Lord's disciples"

(Acts 9:1, REB), God was not only refusing to see only the rage that was in Saul, but also was singling him out for a unique, world-transforming mission in spite of that very rage. Indeed, as Luke goes on to tell us, God drove Saul to his knees and made him a convert of the very gospel that he formerly had denigrated—again, in spite of his rage. From the perspective of our faith, conversion, literally a "turning around" of one's life, is possible even for the most enraged among us with God's help, just as it was for the enraged Saul of Tarsus long ago.

Our task as Christians is to remain always open to the "right moment" for sharing this word of hope, even to those whose rage otherwise arouses in us only fear and contempt. When might that right moment arise? No one can predict. For most enraged people, however, God will create the moment only when *we* are present as God's agents of reconciliation. To be sure, God can do for a criminal on death row what God did directly for Saul. The Deity does not require intermediaries to accomplish the divine purposes; however, our God has also called us to ministry. God asks us to disclose words of grace, redemption, and peace, even to those who may revile the Almighty, themselves, and us while they are listening to our words.

Several months after Patsy's altercation and another's murder, the enraged driver of the pickup truck, Nat, was caught, arrested, and successfully prosecuted. Still later, the young man's mother asked her pastor whether it might be possible for one of the church's lay shepherds to visit her son in prison. After the necessary arrangements were worked out, Darryl began what turned out to be a lengthy series of conversations with Nat at the prison. One included the following exchange:

Darryl: *All of a sudden, Nat, it seems like you're not blaming as many people as you used to for making you mad.*

Nat: *Maybe I've got enough people in here with me to be mad at.*

Darryl: *Somehow I don't think that's quite what the change in you is all about, do you?*

Nat: *Naw, it ain't. Now, I'm just getting mad at myself for being so mad all the time. I can't remember a time when I wasn't mad at somebody over something. And my life hasn't been worth s--- because of it.*

Darryl: *You've got a lot of life still to live.*

Nat: *Yeah, and most of it will be in here; won't it?*

Darryl: *It will; that's for sure. Do you think that means you can't make anything of your life from now on?*

Nat: *What's to make? I'm angry all the time; I've hurt a lot of people; I still hate a lot of them for what they've done to me. I'm nothin' but a pile of s---.*

Darryl: *I don't know about that "nothin' but." You have hurt people, one woman and one man more than anybody ever hurt you. And you still get angry enough to want to keep on hurting people. But there's more to you than that, I believe.*

Nat: *Yeah, sure. Like what?*

Darryl: *Like the Nat who's beginning to see that there's something wrong in him.*

Nat: *A lot of good it's gonna do me. It just makes me feel worse. This place makes you feel bad enough already.*

Darryl: *I believe I know something that might make you feel better.*

Nat: *Give it to me quick.*

Darryl: *The One who made you in the first place hasn't given up on you.*

Nat: *My mom keeps saying that to me, too.*

Darryl: *Do you think she might be right?*

Nat: *I guess I'm at the point now of wantin' to believe she is.*

Darryl: *That's a start!*

Ordinary Christian caring, inspired by faith, love, and prayer, will not be enough in dealing with such extraordinary feelings and expressions of anger as we find in the truly enraged. Nat's anger clearly falls in this category. Even if our personal safety can be fully ensured, we should not attempt to minister to enraged people like Nat all on our own, however strong our Christian commitment may be to witness to God's loving care. They need what God calls us to offer, but they need other kinds of help besides if they are to move beyond a lifestyle dominated by powerful urges to even old and new scores.

For the truly enraged, only treatment under the auspices of a competent mental health professional can possibly suffice to help them in learning to control rage. For those of us who are willing to become caring friends, lay shepherds, or pastors to such persons, such treatment programs can help to create a safe enough context to support the recovery process by our own tangible acts of presence and grace. For others, like Nat, whose rage drives them to commit criminal acts, the only kinds of treatment that society dares offer are those provided in the context of incarceration. Yet in these settings, too, God's loving presence can be mediated through us. After all, did our Lord not expressly communicate to us his expectation that we would visit the imprisoned and that we would do so on a regular basis (Matthew 25:36)?

OVERCOMING HATE

Most morally responsible human beings would find it difficult even to begin sorting out the revolting acts committed by the hate-filled, drunken braggarts described in chapter 2, who beat to death a fellow human being for no other reason than their loathing of his lifestyle. There were five of them, who quickly gathered an admiring coterie of fellow gay-bashers to whom they extolled the righteousness of their deed. Hungrily, the friends feasted on the opportunity to fulfill vicariously their own wishes to obliterate whole groups of people from the face of the earth, from a position of superiority over others defined on their own terms. Had two observers of the scene not become sufficiently repulsed by what they heard to make a report to the police, the murderers might still be free. Now, all are serving life sentences, two without possibility of parole.

Without doubt, a story like this has value as an object lesson on the importance of purging hate from the human heart. But do its gruesome details really have much to do with an exploration of anger in the church? Surely, it is tempting to say, such anger is not the kind we can reasonably expect to encounter among the people in our pews. An insightful fellow parishioner recently summed up the matter for me this way: *People like these are problems for the authorities, not for our pastors and definitely not for us.* What more can be said about this horrific vignette than this?

As a matter of fact, we can and must say a good bit more. Why? By way of an answer, consider the following brief dialogue between an utterly distraught mother, whom I will call Mattie, and her pastor, Karen:

Mattie: *Oh God, oh God, oh God, Karen, it hurts so much that I just want to die, like they made that young man die. We didn't raise those two boys to do something like this! We're God-fearing people, and all we ever wanted from them was to try to lead a good life like we've tried to do. Zack [Mattie's husband] is heartbroken. He can't sleep; he won't eat; he won't talk to nobody. What are we gonna do, Karen? How can we go on, with what our sons and those others did to that poor man? His parents have forgiven us, but how are we ever going to forgive ourselves?*

Karen: *You know deep down that your boys didn't become part of that horrible scene because of anything you did raising them. And yet, you sound like you somehow feel responsible anyway.*

Mattie: *Karen, Zack and I aren't very smart, and we both grew up in pretty rough homes. Our people got mad a lot, they had a lot of bad feelings for folks who weren't like them, and they weren't afraid to show it. We've both got our prejudices; that's for sure. I have to admit that I'm real nervous about all this gay-rights business, and Zack almost comes unglued over it. But kill someone, just because they're not straight? Oh, Karen, you've got to believe me, we never never said anything like that to our boys.*

Karen: *I do believe you, Mattie. The boys may have picked up some of your attitudes and feelings, but I don't think that it was you and Zack who put it into their heads to do what they did.*

As this brief exchange illustrates, some of the most lurid hate crimes that we hear about exhibit a kind of anger that is not as far from our pews as we might like to think. Certainly, in this case, the killers' anger is not "out there" somewhere, a malevolent force defying easy comprehension by Christians who falsely assume that somehow they will never need to come to terms with it. For instance, about a similar occurrence in his own community, one lay leader said to his pastor: *Our people aren't like that. End of discussion.* For him, it was the end of the discussion. For Mattie and Zack, however, the discussion was only beginning because their two boys, now in prison for the rest of their lives, grew up in Karen's church.

Did they begin to learn hate in that church? Might they have heard from its pews or, even worse, from its pulpit that a human being's worth is somehow a function of whether or not he or she belongs to the "right" group or holds the "right" values or is like the rest of us "righteous" people? If so, then they may indeed have become at least partially infected by hate from church people, whom God expects to know better. That we must hold the brothers responsible for their hate-filled actions is not in question. However, we also bear a solemn responsibility as Christians not to pass our personal dislikes and hates along to our children when they are most vulnerable to being affected by them. God calls us to bring any hate-inducing prejudices that we might harbor into the clear light of our Lord's clear admonition to love our enemies and to pray even for those who persecute us.

It is not clear as yet just how people from Karen's church might begin ministering to the two of their own who are in prison for a crime every caregiver can only continue to find abhorrent. Nor is it clear whether the other three men, about whom we know little to nothing, will either accept or even have available to them the ministry of other caring Christians, either from Karen's or another congregation. One thing is clear: those affected by the tragedy, including family members and friends of the murdered young man and of the murderers, have need of Christian shepherding. Each person shocked by this terrible crime, and other violent crimes like them, will have his or her own anger to come to terms with, and the kind of patient understanding that Karen is showing to Mattie can serve as a guide to their own caregivers. In the light of these considerations, we continue the dialogue begun above:

Mattie: *Sometimes I want so bad to get my boys to tell me from their hearts where they got the awful idea that they could do this to anybody.*

Karen: *You haven't asked them about it yet?*

Mattie: *All that Zack and I try to do when we're there with* *either of them is just to tell 'em we don't understand what they did, but we still love 'em and always will.*

Karen: *It's been important to you to give them reassurance.*

Mattie: *Well, sure it has. They haven't got much to look forward to now.*

Karen: *Mattie, I can see that nothing your sons have done will ever diminish the love you have for them. And I hope that your telling them that gives them comfort. But what I'm wondering about is your not sharing with them your feeling of guilt and Zack's sense of shame.*

Mattie: *What good would that do them, on top of everything else they've got to deal with?*

Karen: *I'm more concerned about the good it might do for you. It's awfully hard on you and Zack carrying it all by yourselves. And something else besides.*

Mattie: *What's that?*

Karen: *How angry you must be over what they did, both to that young man and to their own futures.*

Mattie: *I think that if I ever started telling them that, I'd never be able to stop.*

Karen: *I'm sure it seems like that to you, but I also believe that you can find a way to share the feelings that are tearing you up, and still show your sons that you love them.*

We can learn much from this brief sample of Karen's pastoral work with Mattie. First, Karen puts the needs of her care receiver first. Whatever feelings she herself may have about what Mattie's sons have done and the pain their heinous actions have caused so many others, Karen stays focused on what Mattie is saying—and not saying—about her own pain and that of her husband. She both encourages and challenges Mattie to allow the full range of her pain to come to the surface, particularly the anger that Mattie has been hesitant to acknowledge. In this respect, Karen's shepherding provides a good illustration of what Christian ministering can be like when hate invades our pews. Most of our shepherding will be to those affected by others' hate rather than to the hateful perpetrators themselves. There is, then, a good deal of truth in my fellow parishioner's statement that violent wrongdoers must be dealt with primarily (but not exclusively) by those who have both the authority and power to keep us safe from them.

Second, as intensely focused on her parishioner's needs as she is, Karen is also mindful of what Mattie and Zack might do to help their sons come to terms with the enormity of their crime. In other conversations, Karen heard from Mattie and Zack their sons' apologies for hurting them, but she is not convinced that these young men are genuinely remorseful for what they have done to their victim and his family. And, Karen believes, until they come to feel such remorse, the image of God in them can only remain heavily obscured by what Anselm once referred to as "the smoke of wrong-doing." Karen is praying for nothing less than a conversion of the brothers, of which, with God, Mattie and Zack might somehow be its instruments.

The prayers of this wise, young pastor are grounded in a realistic hope that the brothers' present need for parental reassurance may make them more open to facing the full range of the consequences of their behavior if Mattie and Zack can be equipped to express the full range of their own pain as well as their love. Just as it can be helpful to Mattie, in particular, that her sons come to know her feelings both of guilt and of anger, it can be helpful to her sons to realize that they have it in their power to offer as well as to receive reassurance. They can, and should, reassure Mattie and Zack that (1) it is they and not their parents who are at fault and (2) their parents, as well as everyone concerned, have a right to deep anger about what they have done. Both Mattie and Zack have a right to ask this of their sons, and Karen believes that she can help them reach the point of accepting this fact.

Karen is experienced enough as a pastor to know that what she wants Mattie to do from this point on may be something that Mattie herself is not ready to undertake. In this event, Karen will continue to offer her parishioner a sensitive, listening ear and prayers for inner peace in the midst of an otherwise intolerable situation. She will never judge Mattie harshly for resisting or refusing her invitations to approach the situation in other ways. Along the way, though, she will continue to hope and pray for the sons' redemption, through their experiencing both forgiveness and the enormity of that for which God is willing to forgive.

SUMMARY

This chapter has dealt with three forms of anger clearly beyond the range of normal, everyday angry feelings. Fury, rage, and hate are not easily manageable, but we still bear responsibility for controlling them and for ensuring that they do not lead us and others into harm.

The Christian perspective on anger earlier described in this book, with its emphasis on learning to be angry for the right reasons, is especially challenged by the pervasiveness of anger that seems so clearly to be for all the wrong reasons. Even more disturbing is the indisputable fact that fury, rage, and hate also can manifest themselves in people who should always know better: the people in our pews, even ourselves. Within all of us, however, is power to overcome furious outbursts, enraged impulses to retaliate against others all out of proportion to their offenses, and smoldering hatred of groups whose differences from us displease us. It is the gracious, loving power of God, continuing to make all things new.

8 Staying Angry for the Right Reasons

F ROM THE PERSPECTIVE OF FAITH, THE TRIVIAL AND HURTFUL anger that even the most committed Christians sometimes feel and express serves little, if any, useful purpose. One kind of anger, however, exists for good reasons, and from it all our relationships can and often do change for the better. This kind of anger, righteous anger, is the central focus of everything that our Lord taught about feeling and expressing anger in the ways that God intends. As such, it is worthy both of our respect and our cultivation. How to make genuinely righteous anger a continuing spiritual concern is the principal subject of this final chapter.

ANGER THAT REDEEMS

Becoming angry for the right reasons, or "for cause," has to do with reacting to the deprivation of something basic to our own or another's well-being and even survival. God does not intend for our reactions to such deprivations to become the primary focus of attention. Merely dwelling on the deprivations, and fanning our anger about them, will only plunge us into a perpetual state of resentful, hopeless protests against evils we delude ourselves into believing we can do nothing about. Rather, God intends for us to let our indignation provide the motivation and energy we need to persist in addressing the deprivations until we make some contribution to their alleviation. Like every other kind of anger, righteous anger cannot be worked through by "nursing" it for its own sake; it requires constructive action.

Between our recognition of a significant deprivation and our feeling righteous anger about it, there is also activated within us one or more strongly held convictions about what kinds of things should and should not happen to people in our world. For Christians, these convictions are likely to represent the heart of personal faith. The perceived incongruity between the deprivation before us and those convictions influences decisively how intense our righteous anger will be and how hard we will work to get at its source, whether in our own lives or in the lives of others. The more flagrant the contradiction between what we believe should be happening to people and what we see actually happening to them, the deeper our anger is likely to go, the longer it is likely to endure, and the more motivating it is likely to be of constructive action on our part.

The kinds of convictions that so clearly shape the feeling of righteous anger can be expressed in many different ways, as the following statements show:

The harassment that has been so much a part of this department has to stop.

I'm worthy of more attention than I'm getting from my supervisor.

No one deserves the kind of abuse that he has had to take from those parents.

While we take fertile land out of production, children are starving all around the world. Surely, Christians have a responsibility to do something about this situation.

If we really mean what we say about equal opportunity, we are going to have to do more about leveling the playing field for everyone from the start.

A small number of people at the top are getting richer, while a large number of people at the bottom are getting poorer. This can in no way be fair.

Abortion as a means of contraception is no more justified

than war is as an instrument of national policy.
How can we live with ourselves when we don't get the vac-
cines that people need to them—whether or not their coun-
tries can pay for them?
How long are people going to keep on killing each other in
the name of religion?
We deserve better than to have our homes broken into time
and time again.

Not a list of normative beliefs that should be accepted unquestion-
ingly by everyone, these statements illustrate the kinds of convictions
that do influence peoples' becoming deeply angry about significant
deprivations that they strongly believe no one ought to suffer. Some
of the statements are patently controversial. Together, however, they
remind us that each of us has a God-given right to think and believe
what makes sense to us as individuals. For the sake of the communities of faith that God intends for us, though, we also have an obligation to subject even our most cherished personal convictions to continuing examination. The best way to do this is through discussion
with others, who often see better than we do whether a particular
conviction makes good sense or not.

What these considerations imply most fundamentally for our relationships is that it is always possible to disagree with one another over
basic beliefs about the world and our place in it. We must learn to
accept such disagreements without becoming overly angry about
them and without allowing them to diminish in any way our respect
for those who disagree with us. They are as important to God as we
are. People, even loving members of the same community of faith, can
disagree about basic beliefs on the basis of principle; that is, they can
question the truth of a belief itself. By way of example, consider the
statement about the rich getting richer and the poor getting poorer. Is
this description about the economy of our country true? Some ana-
lysts say yes, while others say no. Possibilities for disagreement also
arise over the relevance of a belief to a particular set of circumstances.
For example, two people might agree with the description of the
economy but disagree over whether this amounts to treating people
unfairly and, therefore, over whether any kind of remedial action is

called for at all. The fact that we disagree with one another from time to time about what should and should not happen in the world does not alter the basic point that feeling righteous anger always requires the activation of some core belief.

The process of managing and controlling most kinds of anger is one that begins with getting angry about some real deprivation and perceiving its incongruity with a belief about what we and other people should and should not have to endure. It ends with our taking relevant action to overcome the deprivation itself, hopefully without bringing further harm to ourselves or others. More often than not, this process leads to a satisfactory resolution of a great deal of our anger, either by helping us to attain something important that we or someone else previously lacked or to accept the necessity of prolonged frustration in its absence. Righteous anger, however, does not yield as easily to this process.

WHY RIGHTEOUS ANGER DOES NOT GO AWAY

As the Old Testament reminds us frequently, the ancient prophets of Israel constantly made themselves thorns in the sides of their nation's leaders and, more often than not, of the people as well. They were relentless in representing both the strident demands and glorious promises of an uncompromising God, hurling self-doubt and the pain of others' denunciation, along with fears of persecution and death, into a fiery furnace of their own seething anger and transporting visions of national rebirth. These strange and disturbing prophets of old continue to inspire our respect and gratitude. However, candor requires us to admit that they elicit affection no more from us than they did from their own people.

Then and now, righteously angry people unflinchingly raise the hackles of even their strongest admirers. Their intensity and single-mindedness, even when in the service of an undeniably just cause, can become offensive and wearying. In the mysterious working of God, those who bear the burden of forging others' diffuse moral sensitivities into guiding images of a better world seem to suffer more than a fair share of their generation's ridicule and rejection. In spite of our own best intentions, we, too, sometimes lose patience with righteously angry family members, friends, and leaders. We press them to soften both their anger and their convictions. As one frustrated husband I know told his social activist wife one day: *It's time you stopped trying to change the world and come back home to the people who really love you and need you.* It is easy to understand and even appreciate this husband's impatience. However, even if his wife wants to respond positively to his plea, it is not likely that she can so respond, because she believes that if she does accede, she will become less than the kind of person God wants her to be. From deep within her soul, and to the consternation of those who love her the most, this anguished homemaker grasps firmly one of the most fundamental truths about righteous anger: if we temper it, we will become as hopeless about changing things as are the men and women whose deprivations evoke it in the first place.

Is moderating righteous anger this difficult? After all, it is tempting to say, anger is anger, and how we deal with all our other feelings of anger surely should hold for those rare instances in which we put people off by indignation over newly discovered wrongs. With regard to such indignation, is not the most constructive response simply that of alleviating the deprivation fueling it? The answer to this question is an unsettling yes and no. On the one hand, we must never let our zeal for action lose stamina in the face of human need. On the other hand, however, righteous anger, unlike other kinds of anger, is relatively impervious to dissolution by means of specific actions, no matter how well-intentioned those actions may be, because righteous anger is aroused by a different kind of deprivation than most of the ones encountered thus far in this book.

At the heart of all righteous anger are *core deprivations,* which are deeply embedded in what for the Christian tradition is a "fallen" world, a world deformed by our own pride-filled, destructive behaviors that perpetually seek to usurp the place of our Creator in the scheme of things. Core deprivations persist across many different societies and civilizations, over generations, centuries, and millennia. They work their devastation in spite of humanity's best efforts to overcome them. Many examples of such deprivations have been given throughout this book; to those should be added the conditions of grinding poverty, mass starvation, ethnic and cultural genocide, wholesale abridgements of human rights and liberties, and to-the-death competition for exclusive possession and control of the earth's many resources that rightly belong to everyone. The power of conditions like these to overwhelm individuals, families, and whole societies has made the world a very hostile environment for the majority of people throughout recorded history. These are not the conditions God envisions for us. Rather, they are what we have made of things because we continue to repudiate our responsibilities before God and put our own interests first.

Those who grasp the fallenness of our world—its distorted, deformed character that is the product of human beings substituting their own plans for God's—and who hold fast to a vision of how much better our world can be than it now is are especially vulnerable to righteous anger. Like fury, rage, and hate, righteous anger is intense and not easily deflected. Unlike them, however, righteous anger does not subvert our powers to perceive things accurately, to make good judgments about them, and to act responsibly toward all of God's creatures. Its perdurability derives precisely from the clarity with which the justifiably indignant see what is really going on from the vantage point of a higher moral and spiritual vision. The prophet Micah gives us an especially powerful example of what such a moral and spiritual vision is like:

> *He hath shown thee, O man, what is good; and what doth*
> *the* LORD *require of thee, but to do justly, and to love mercy,*
> *and to walk humbly with thy God? (Micah 6:8, KJV)*

CELEBRATING THE GIFT OF RIGHTEOUS ANGER

However unsettling righteously angry people may be, their capacity to feel anger toward and to seek redress of wrongs in the world is one of God's greatest gifts to them and to us as well. Rather than our criticism and our judgment, they need and deserve our appreciation and support. We can render this appreciation and support most especially by (1) honoring their gift of discernment and the anger that inevitably must accompany it, (2) listening closely enough to create opportunities for them to assess their anger objectively, (3) guiding

them toward more effective ways of expressing their anger constructively, and (4) encouraging them when their energy is at a low
ebb. Accompanying any and all of these expressions should be
constant prayer with and for them that their feelings and actions
will bear fruit.

We can say many kinds of things to honor righteous anger in the
lives of family members, friends, and care receivers; for example:

*How could you not be angry over our mother's drinking her-
self to death?*

*You're worried about how angry you get over what your father
did to your sister and you when you were little. I'm with you in
trying to figure out how to forgive him. But you know what? It
was a terrible thing he did, and I don't believe that God could
be put out with you for feeling the way you do.*

*Yeah, it looks like it would be risky to blow the whistle on
those guys. Your anger about what they're doing, though, is
telling you something; isn't it? It's telling you that you know
they're doing something wrong and that somehow they need
to be stopped.*

*No matter how hard you and the team tries, you just can't
keep the drug dealers off these streets. I'm giving thanks to
God, though, that you're still riled up about it, because that
says you're not giving up.*

It is a good thing to feel angry about self-destructive behaviors,
abuse, cheating, and leading others to harm. It is a good thing to feel
angry about injustice of every kind. God intends for us to feel angry
about such things and for our anger to give us the energy we need to
change them for the better. Shepherding people who struggle for less
dysfunctional families, better working conditions, safer neighborhoods, equal opportunity for all, integrity and vitality in our churches—in other words, for a commonwealth of peace, good will, mutual support, and hope for the future—need all the affirmation we can
give them. The affirmation properly begins by honoring the anger
that societal evils inspire in them, especially when others begin to tell
them in not-so-subtle ways that getting along by going along is the
more acceptable course.

Sometimes, however, it may not be possible to honor the angry feelings that another shares with us and maintain our integrity. For example, many today who are engaged in struggles for justice seem to be as angry with oppressors as a group as some of the oppressors within a particular group are with those whom they exploit. But not everyone who is assigned the hated category of "oppressor"—for example, whether male, white, Western, straight, or rich—is part of the problem. Instead, some are actually working on its solution. Being angry with someone without knowing just where that person stands regarding the issue in question is not something we can justifiably praise. What we can do is listen to the persons expressing the anger, in the hope that our listening might help them to discover for themselves if their anger has gotten them off track.

Good listening is especially warranted when we have doubts about the genuineness of another's outwardly righteous anger. It can help us assess whether we understand the other accurately and to establish the trust needed if we decide to challenge him or her in some way. How might we raise the issue of genuineness with someone who is angry about something that everyone should be angry about but whose anger nevertheless seems to be serving more selfish than self-less purposes? One way is to tell the person what we think he or she needs to be told and then to let the chips fall where they may. A more productive approach is to respect the other person's understanding of his or her experiences and to offer timely invitations to look at those experiences in other ways. The following exchange provides an illustration of how respectful listening can stimulate new thinking about feelings and actions:

Mary: *So it's beginning to get you down, all the bureaucratic infighting.*

Charlotte: *It really is, Mary. You can't believe what you have to go through these days just to get a little food and some clothes to homeless people downtown. The city gets after us, our church's board constantly carps about what we're doing, my family is resentful of the time I'm putting in, and on and on.*

Mary: *What keeps you going?*

Charlotte: *Oh, a couple of things, I guess. I stay mad at all*

the comfortable people I know who don't care anything about the less fortunate and who won't lift a finger to help them.
Mary: *You said a couple of things.*
Charlotte: *Well, there are those wonderful expressions on the faces of the people we bring things to. They are so grateful to us.*
Mary: *All of them?*
Charlotte: *No, not all. Some people almost grab the things right out of our hands and walk off without saying even a word of thanks.*
Mary: *How does that make you feel?*
Charlotte: *Like going up to them and giving them a good piece of my mind.*
Mary: *Now you sound almost as mad as you did when you were talking about the city and the church board.*
Charlotte: *Well, everybody needs to feel appreciated; don't they?*
Mary: *I sure don't know anybody who doesn't. But I also wonder some about how much appreciation is enough.*
Charlotte: *Do you think I may be asking for too much?*
Mary: *You'd know better than I would about that. To me, it just seems important to keep on asking that kind of question.*
Charlotte: *Maybe I'm doing all this more for the gratitude I get from it than I've wanted to believe.*
Mary: *Maybe so. What impresses me, though, is how you stick to it even when you feel underappreciated.*
Charlotte: *I really believe that what we're doing is important. I guess what I need to work on is griping less and enjoying it more.*
Mary: *That's a winning combination to me.*

Another situation will illustrate unhelpful and helpful expressions of concern about another's genuineness. Donnie, who is very active in social causes, is relishing the notice he has been getting lately from the media in his community. The adulation seems to have become more important to him than the good he accomplishes. Even one of his closest friends wonders whether his angry protests intend to call more attention to himself than to those he says he wants to help. Thus far, this friend has kept his thoughts to himself. Two of Donnie's other friends, Stu and Harv, have not. Stu's approach shuts down the conversation immediately:

Stu: *You keep on saying how outraged you are, but, Donnie, I'm getting in your face to tell you that all you've got is a swelled head. You're loving the ego trip, but you aren't getting close to the people who are suffering.*

Donnie: *Man, you're just gettin' jealous of me all of a sudden. That's all this is about; isn't it?*

Harv chooses to go about things differently, with a much better result:

Harv: *You're telling me that you get a huge high from doing what you're doing. Willing to say a little more about what that high is like?*

Donnie: *It's just been a trip, Harv, walking through these streets and having everybody call me by name. Nobody down here used to know me at all. It's better than drugs!*

Harv: *A lot of what you're saying is beginning to worry me a little.*

Donnie: *What do you mean?*

Harv: *I know you're not doing drugs, but I'm worrying that you like being liked so much.*

Donnie: *Yeah, I guess I ought to be worried about it, too. I'm beginning to sound like a real punk. How did I get to the point of feeling so good about myself when other people are hurtin' so bad?*

Premature judgment of someone engaged in a righteous cause is likely to bring dialogue to an end rather than to open it up. By contrast, a caring friend's active, inquisitive listening goes a long away toward helping an angry person discover what her or his anger is really all about and whether its basis is moral sensitivity, personal pique, or self-aggrandizement. It also lays the groundwork for the third way of expressing appreciation and support of righteously angry people: guiding.

Guiding, offered by someone who cares, is especially needed when, and for whatever reason, the constructive expression of righteous anger becomes difficult. Sometimes, people who are angry for good reason do not translate their anger effectively into the kinds of action that could do some good. Instead, they allow it to churn within them, like chronic complaining more than justifiable indignation. In such situations, we may find it appropriate, and even necessary, to say things like the following:

- *You've been mad at them for a long time, for good reason. What about taking some action against them?*
- *You're angrier than most people about that company's waste dumping because you've seen the results with your own eyes. You've helped me to understand the situation better, and I appreciate that. And maybe that's all you should be doing with your anger right now. I can't help thinking, though, that you might be doing a lot more. Any ideas?*
- *Brother, I hear you talking the talk, but it's one thing to holler and shout that things aren't right, and another to make them right. You know a lot more about what we can do than I know. What about working on getting something done instead of just griping?*

The common theme running through all these statements is that righteous anger is more than a way merely to fulminate against evil; it is a resource for resisting and transforming it.

If some righteously angry people keep too much of their anger in for too long, others want to pour it out too soon, indiscriminately, and as a consequence get in their own way of dealing with the offending causes. Besides encountering such people in our own daily rounds, we often learn about them from others' comments:

- *That gal really gave it to us straight on, and I know we needed to hear it. But, wow, by the time she got through, the committee was so put out with her that they weren't going to take any kind of action anyhow, anyway. I know it's wrong for us to be this way, but isn't there somebody around who can make these same points less offensively?*
- *Our preacher learned his lessons well in seminary about afflicting the comfortable. He's right that we're too comfortable, but some of us could stand a little more love from him, along with what he's trying to teach us.*

- *When he got through laying out all his criticisms of us, I couldn't even feel mad anymore. I just felt rotten. I'm ready to pack it in.*

We might say a number of things to the overly zealous by way of helping them to be more effective in what they believe they and others should be doing; for example:

- *Part of me wants to say, "You go, gal!" about what you said to the committee. But the other part of me is really sad that they wound up doing nothing at all about the situation. As you think about it now, does anything occur to you that you might have said or done differently to bring about a better outcome?*
- *[with a grin] Pastor, I've taught Sunday school classes about Amos. I know him well. And, brother, you're no Amos! [more seriously] If you let us know that you respect us and will be there for us no matter what, you'll get a lot further helping us to become a more socially concerned church.*
- *There's got to be a better way to turn this thing around than just making people feel guilty and bad about themselves. If we keep going on like this, we'll eventually defeat our own purposes and programs, even though we know we're right. Any ideas?*

People who are angry about core deprivations need more than our honoring, listening, and guiding. They also need our encouragement during the long, inevitable periods of discouragement in which indignation can easily turn into despair. In the sin-ridden world in which we live, things to outrage perceptive people with high ideals will always exist, and initial anger about those things may not be strong enough to sustain the arduous work of changing what needs to be changed. What can help are copious expressions of gratitude and even admiration; for example:

- *Even though it's hard for you to be hopeful that things are going to change much, you still believe that it's important to stand up and be counted. You're an inspiration to a lot of people right now. You do know that; don't you?*

- *I respect you for not throwing in the towel.*
- *Things have been like this longer than anybody can remember, and they aren't going to go away overnight. Remember that while you keep on fighting, and don't ever forget that you're fighting for the right things.*

It is not easy to be consistently encouraging of peoples' efforts to translate righteous anger into positive and effective action. The single-mindedness of the truly righteous can wear out the patience of even the most patient caregiver, who may finally blurt out something like, *Can't we ever talk about something else, even for just a little while?* Expressing our frustration this way, however, only puts our own anger ahead of the care receiver's. One lay shepherd, weary of what she called her zealous care receiver's "tunnel vision," nevertheless found a better way to keep her lines of communication open:

It looks like we've said about all there is to say on this matter for now. Could we revisit it when we get together next time? You've mentioned other concerns in your life these days, and I'm wondering whether we might look at one of those before we stop for today.

SUMMARY

People who feel keenly the kind of anger that religious prophets of old exemplified are deserving of a special kind of caring that is patient, supportive, sometimes confrontative, but most importantly, long-suffering. The core deprivations that truly righteous anger discloses are deeper and more encompassing than the insults and injuries we suffer individually in our personal relationships, painful and undeserved as these, too, may be. Core deprivations go to the very conditions of human existence and well-being in the world, and the struggle to overcome them can never be easy. Those who engage in the struggle often sacrifice something of what otherwise might be a more pleasant countenance and demeanor. They deserve more from us, however, than our being put off by their single-minded devotion. They deserve our gratitude, our admiration, and, most especially, our love.

Appendix

Some Questions to Think About

OR THE SAKE OF MANAGING ANGER MORE EFFECTIVELY, IT IS VITALLY important that we understand the nature and the roots of our angry feelings, whenever those feelings occur. In sum, we need to know what our anger is about. Anger is a very powerful feeling. It can easily overwhelm our capacities for clear thinking and responsible decision-making, and provoke us to impulsive and potentially harmful reactions to the slightest offenses—at the expense of even our most cherished relationships. The power of anger deserves our serious respect, even as we strive to channel that power toward constructive ends.

By understanding how and why we become angry, we can direct our anger toward successful resolution of the frustrations that contribute to it in the first place. Even more importantly, such understanding can help us develop more compassion toward ourselves and others for the angry feelings that are the inevitable accompaniment of most human striving. With compassion, we can better help ourselves and others deal with anger in ways that are pleasing to God.

Because the effective management of anger begins with ourselves, we must be willing to engage in serious and sustained self-reflection as the foundation of understanding both our own anger and that of others. By "*self*-reflection," I mean two things in particular here. First, self-reflection involves *attentiveness* to what is going on within us at the level of our own feelings, and with that attentiveness must be a corresponding interest in discovering the roots of those feelings and what we should do about them. Second, self-reflection involves *examination* of the convictions we hold about how things are and should be—with a corresponding commitment to subject those convictions to continuous evaluation. This appendix is devoted to the end of facilitating self-reflection, in both these senses of the term.

The material that follows is a series of questions inviting readers to think more deeply about their feelings of anger and concerning their convictions about the world which elicit that anger, all in relation to the insights and issues each chapter of this book introduces. In my judgment, the best way to make use of these questions is by writing responses to them in a personal journal upon the completion of the chapter to which the questions are linked. These personal responses might then be discussed in a small-group setting or in one-on-one counseling.

CHAPTER 1: INTRODUCTION

1. Are there angry people in *your* church? Are you one of them? What are they/you angriest about? Do they/you have good reason(s) to be as angry as they/you are? Why or why not?

2. What kinds of conflict do you believe are (a) inevitable in any congregation, whether helpful or not, (b) potentially helpful to strengthening at least some congregations, and (c) almost always destructive to any congregation? Why do you categorize each issue as you have done?

3. How well does your congregation deal with internal dissension and conflict among its members? Do you believe that the process is generally effective? If so, what do you think contributes most to its effectiveness? If not, how might things be improved? What role might you play in such improvements?

CHAPTER 2: THE MANY FACES OF ANGER

1. When you were growing up, what kinds of anger were most often expressed between (a) other members of your family, (b) family members and you, and (c) you and your friends?

2. When someone gets angry with you now, (a) how do you typically feel, and (b) what do you typically do? Has it always been like this for you? Why or why not?

3. What kinds of anger do you find hardest to accept in others? What would you have to do within yourself in order to be helpful to those types of angry people?

4. From your experiences to this point in your life, what are the most important lessons that you have learned about expressing your own anger?

CHAPTER 3: IS THERE A "CHRISTIAN" FACE OF ANGER?

1. From (a) Christian family members, (b) people active in the church, and (c) the church itself, what messages have you received about getting angry and about dealing with feelings of anger?

2. Without naming names, describe briefly the angriest person you know in the pews of your own church. Why is he or she so angry? Is the anger consistent with being a good Christian? Why or why not? What, in your judgment, would be the best way to help this person deal with his or her anger?

3. If one of your children or grandchildren asked you, "Why does God get so mad so much?" how would you answer?

4. For you, to what extent is God (a) an angry God, and (b) a loving God? Have you always believed what you now believe about this? What and/or who has most influenced your thinking on the subject?

CHAPTER 4: HOW AND WHY WE GET ANGRY

1. About what kinds of things do you get the most angry? What helps you most in managing this anger?

2. In what ways, if any, has life treated you (a) fairly, (b) more than fairly, (c) unfairly, and (d) really, really unfairly?

3. How often do you (a) count your blessings and give thanks for them, (b) dwell on the bad things that have happened to you, and (c) wish that things had worked out differently for you?

4. For the most part, are you satisfied with your life? If so, what has contributed most to the satisfaction you now experience? If not, how do you deal with the frustration you may be feeling about things?

5. What are the most important deprivations you have so far experienced in life? How have you dealt with them in the past? How do you deal with them now?

CHAPTER 5: DEALING WITH EVERYDAY ANGER

1. If you have not already done so, write out answers to the ten questions asked on pages 55 and 56 of the book.

2. Describe briefly your most recent feeling of anger toward someone or something. Did anything constructive come from the anger you felt? If so, what? If not, why not?

CHAPTER 6: GETTING BEYOND GRUDGES AND PAYBACKS

1. Have you ever held a grudge against someone? If so, what was it about? Did the issue ever get resolved? How? If not, what do you do to prevent yourself from turning irritations and frustrations into grudges?

2. Have you ever felt like seeking revenge on someone? If so, why? Did you act on the feeling? Why or why not?

3. Have you ever been a victim of someone else's desire for revenge? If so, how did/do you feel about it and respond to it? If not, how do you manage to avoid arousing such a desire in others?

4. From the standpoint of our faith, what justification, if any, might there be for retaliating against someone who has committed an offensive or harmful act? If you believe there is justification for retaliating in some instances, what form should the retaliation take?

CHAPTER 7: TOWARD THE EXTREMES: FURY, RAGE, AND HATE

1. Have you ever lost your temper with someone or over something? If so, what was the issue? What form did your loss of temper take? At the time, was there a good reason for your anger? If you do not remember losing your temper yourself, how do you feel generally toward people who do not manage their own tempers well?

2. What steps do you believe our society should take to bring more violent forms of anger under better control?

3. What do you believe to be the most serious forms of prejudice facing human beings today? How can we overcome such prejudice, as individuals and as a society?

4. What do you believe to be the principal causes of criminal behavior in today's society? What do you think are the best solution(s) to the contemporary problem of crime?

CHAPTER 8: STAYING ANGRY FOR THE RIGHT REASONS

1. What do you understand to be the "right" and the "wrong" reasons for getting and staying angry?

2. As you think about your own angriest moments, describe one or two that illustrate getting angry (a) for the "right" reasons and (b) for the "wrong" reasons. Describe a scenario in which it is possible to be angry for the "right" reasons—but to express that anger in "wrong" ways.

3. Is there anything you would now like to change about the way you experience and express anger, and/or about the way you deal with other peoples' anger? If so, what? How could you best make the changes you want to make?

4. What do you believe our churches should be the most angry about today? What actions might your church take to respond to those anger-inspiring issues?

For those who read this book for personal enrichment, the "journaling" I have recommended for the questions above will go a long way toward guiding them to find in its pages concrete help in managing their own anger more effectively. Journaling will also prove to be a useful part of study and training courses that congregations may choose to initiate based on the book.

In the latter case, I have found most rewarding a course format that devotes 60–90 minutes to each of the chapters over a four to six week period, with each session including summary and discussion of the chapter material. These sessions should also allot time for sharing from the personal journals of the participants, as group members become willing to contribute. How the time of each session is distributed between discussing the chapter material and sharing from members' journals will depend upon the group's own interest in combination with the stated aim of the study (e.g., general interest; personal growth; training for caregiving; etc.). Along with weekly meetings, an all-day, weekend retreat will enhance group members' overall experience of dealing with the material and with their own experiences of anger, in themselves and in others.